101 Campaign Tips For
Women Candidates and Their Staffs

by

Jewel Lansing

Foreword by

Congresswoman Jolene Unsoeld

101 Campaign Tips For Women Candidates And Their Staffs

Copyright © 1991 by Jewel Lansing

Published by

R&E Publishers
P.O. Box 2008
Saratoga, CA 95070
Phone: (408) 866-6303
Fax: (408) 866-0825

I.S.B.N. 0-88247-886-9
Library of Congress 91-52961

Cover Design by Janet Simmonds
Typesetting by Diane Parker

Dedication: To women candidates of yesterday, today and tomorrow.

NOTE: The 101 tips in this book are keyed to the text of a companion book which is being published concurrently. *Campaigning for Office: A Woman Runs* is a first-person account of a woman running for statewide office at a time when none had yet been elected to such office in Oregon.

FOREWORD

Elected officials bring unique perspectives to the issues they face—perspectives based on the experiences they've had and the lives they've led. In order for our democracy to be truly representative, it is important to elect people who reflect the diversity of our nation.

Yet women are vastly underrepresented at all levels of our political process. From a low of 2 percent of the U.S. Senate to a high of 18 percent of state legislatures, women's voices make up a small percentage of those heard in town halls, city council chambers, state capitols, governors' mansions, and the U.S. Capitol.

That's why it is so important for more women to run for and win elective office, and for those of us who have made it to continue to speak out on issues that have touched our lives. In the first few months of the 102nd Congress, I can think of many examples of Congresswomen's personal experiences impacting on the legislation we faced:

- As Democratic members worked on the Civil Rights Act of 1991, Eleanor Holmes Norton, an African-American woman who came to Congress with years of experience as a civil rights attorney, was a very effective advocate. She could explain not only what the bill was designed to do, but also the experiences she has had and seen which make this bill necessary.

- When a Congresswoman returned to the floor of the House after having surgery to remove a cancerous lump from her breast, the first topic she addressed was funding for breast cancer research. While men can be empathetic, they can never know what it's like to have a yearly mammogram, or to face the anguish that women living with breast cancer are confronting right now.

- Hours after the Supreme Court announced the *Rust vs. Sullivan* decision upholding the administration's "gag rule" for health care practitioners in federally funded family planning clinics, Congresswoman Nita Lowey had pulled together a press conference to denounce the ruling. Seven other women members of Congress joined her in calling for legislation to ban the enforcement of this rule.

Men can be effective advocates for all of these issues—and many of them are. But it's time that more women start speaking for themselves on these and other issues facing our nation.

Running for office is difficult, and winning is even more difficult. But by working together and sharing our experiences, the process becomes easier. I would encourage anyone who is considering a run for public office to read about other women's successes and failures so we can learn through each other.

--Congresswoman Jolene Unsoeld

ACKNOWLEDGMENTS

The inspiration to expand these guidelines, originally an appendix to *Campaigning for Office: A Woman Runs*, came from James Anderson, former publisher of Breitenbush Books. His encouragement, enthusiasm and vision convinced me to solicit anecdotes and examples from women's campaigns across the country and incorporate them into a book of hard-nosed advice for female candidates.

I acknowledge with thanks the many authors, candidates, political consultants, advisors, books, journals and articles identified in the text and appendix to this book. I also utilized election and political coverage from the *Daily Oregonian*, various newspapers, and several weekly news magazines.

Women candidates who helped shape the original guidelines were Betty Roberts, Norma Paulus, Caren Adams, Joyce Cohen, Susan Graber, Jane Cease, Bev Stein, Susan Sokol-Blosser, Gretchen Kafoury, and Lisa Naito. Other individuals who provided assistance and information regarding this book included Marie Morse, Maura Breuger, Rebecca Tillet, Iris Portny, Sheila Lawrence, Harriet Garrett, Linda Fletcher, Judi Roman, Joan Smith, Joyce Bay, Nancy Mitchell, Kathryn Falk, Jamie Cooper, Jennifer Gamblin, Molly Hunter, Sara Carlin Ames, Jennifer Treat, Phyllis Oster, Gina Whitehill Baziuk, Mary Legry, Bob Crane, Deborah Kafoury, Jann Phenix, Dan Evans, Bill Cryer, and members of my Clackamas writers' critique group.

I am deeply indebted to the busy political consultants, campaign managers, past and future candidates, and interested observers from various parts of the country who read this manuscript in draft form and made suggestions for improvements. My sincerest thanks to Cathy Allen, Julie Williamson, Gary Blackmer, Cheryl Copeland, Wendy Sherman, Frances Shipman, Thalia Zepatos, Ann Porter, Sharon Little, Nancy Rangila, Darlene Hooley, Betsy Johnson, JoAnne Nordling, Margaret Davies and Alyse Lansing Gass. Some of the words in this book are theirs, but I take full responsibility for the selection and presentation of the contents.

My strongest motivation in writing this book has been the hope that thousands of women will someday be elected to office with the help of the practical advice, theory, examples and common sense squeezed into these pages.

Jewel Beck Lansing
Portland, Oregon
June 1991

CONTENTS

Tips 1-18: THE DECISION TO RUN

1. Visualize yourself in the role of candidate for months, even years, before you run.

2. Find a political mentor.

3. Assess your strengths and weaknesses for becoming a candidate.

4. Be sure you have the "fire in your belly" to run.

5. Seek an office with no incumbent to increase your chances of winning.

6. Become a proven vote getter to position yourself as a viable candidate for higher office.

7. Be in top physical condition before embarking upon a campaign.

8. Activate your campaign nine months to a year before a primary.

9. Know the office you're aspiring to and the election laws governing your race.

10. Consider touching base with your hometown editor before making a final commitment to enter a major race.

11. Contact friends, acquaintances, prominent persons and potential contributors for support and advice before you declare.

12. Consider withdrawing before filing deadline to keep your name off the ballot if your chances of making a decent showing are nil.

13. Don't assume that organizations you belong to or whose principles you espouse will automatically support you.

14. Don't underestimate the effect of your candidacy on your co-workers, clients, employees and friends.

15. Evaluate statewide and congressional races differently from county and legislative contests.

16. Educate the public about participation in democracy as one of your campaign goals.

17. Expect the unexpected; happenstance is part of the game of politics.

18. Recognize that deciding when and if to run is the hardest, and most important, decision you will make.

Tips 19-30: MONEY AND FUND RAISING

19. Do not underestimate the need for money!

20. Face the fact that you must be a salesperson to raise needed funds for a campaign.

21. Decide the limits of your family financial support, whether or not you can tolerate unpaid debts, and how expenditure commitments will be monitored.

22. Scrutinize the budget your campaign manager proposes; the primary burden of raising the money to meet its goals will be yours.

23. Find a financial angel.

24. Get "in-kind" contributions to keep cash outlay down; securing free headquarters space should be a high priority.

25. Ask everyone for money; no one gives unless they're asked.

26. Be prepared for a fund-raising event at which nobody shows.

27. Project the image of a winner; people contribute to WINNING campaigns.

28. Have cash on hand to pay for media buys well in advance.

29. Outspend your opponent; winning candidates almost always do.

30. Meet, during non-election years, with corporate executives who give money to other political candidates.

Tips 31-35: CAMPAIGN STRUCTURE
AND THE CAMPAIGN MANAGER

31. Give highest priority to choosing a campaign manager.

32. Set parameters for how much or how little you will personally be involved in the details of the campaign.

33. Decide what purpose and role your steering committee will play before you ask people to serve; keep authority for campaign policy decisions within a tight circle of three to five people.

34. Consider hiring a political consultant with broad campaign authority.

35. Expect some staff and volunteer turnover early in the campaign.

Tips 36-45: CAMPAIGN MANAGEMENT

36. Design a top-notch written campaign plan.

37. Learn the business of campaigning as you would any other enterprise in which you have invested thousands of dollars.

38. Allow enough lead time for preparation of activities and events, and details which precede them, such as drafts of solicitation letters, printing, etc.

39. Be prepared for invisible campaign work to eat up chunks of time, both for you and your staff.

40. Convert your knowledge of potential supporters onto a large computer base.

41. Delegate responsibility for scheduling your time to only one person.

42. Know that most people wait to be asked before volunteering their services to a campaign.

43. Demonstrate your appreciation of enthusiastic and committed volunteers; they can influence a race dramatically.

44. Sign thank-you letters to contributors and volunteers personally.

45. Don't expect your campaign to run perfectly.

Tips 46-59: CANDIDATE OBLIGATIONS AND OPPORTUNITIES

46. Have a clear explanation of your motivation for running rehearsed and fluent.

47. Learn public speaking. Enjoy it. Practice, practice, practice.

48. Find yourself a full-time driver-aide for a major race.

49. Be well prepared for your first joint appearance with your opponent; it will set the tone of the whole campaign.

50. Understand that you will need to be waited upon—an especially difficult lesson for women candidates, their families, and staffs to learn.

51. Notify the person in charge when you arrive at political functions, whether or not you are scheduled as a speaker.

52. Develop a methodology for capturing on-the-spot information you receive on the campaign trail, such as names, addresses, and reason for contacting.

53. Value TIME as your most precious possession.

54. Be cautious about appearing anywhere with a male other than your spouse, campaign manager, or a campaign official.

55. Assume that each new audience knows nothing about you or your race or the issues.

56. Clarify who can speak for you and who can't.

57. Find ego-boosters to keep your spirits up, to make you feel like a million dollars.

58. Smile. Relax. Be yourself.

59. Expect election day to be the longest day of your life.

Tips 60-71: STRATEGY

60. Calculate how many votes you will need to win and have a strategy for winning them, geographically and by methodology.

61. Identify constituency groups which have a vested interest in who gets elected to your office.

62. Do polling in every major race.

63. Be prepared to deal with gender as a factor in political races for the foreseeable future.

64. Make name familiarity and raising money your main campaign goals.

65. Seek endorsements religiously.

66. Realize that your advertising agency can make or break your campaign.

67. Focus scarce advertising dollars on complete penetration by one or two media rather than trying to do everything.

68. Find one low-cost piece of campaign paraphernalia (Buttons? Bumper stickers? Window decals?) plus a brochure, for mass production.

69. Count on party support and that of other office holders in your party once nominated in a partisan primary.

70. Avoid endorsing other candidates when you are in a close race; you don't need anyone else's baggage.

71. Be prepared for difficult and constant scheduling and cancelling choices.

Tips 72-76: ISSUES

72. Know that people vote FOR candidates they trust and AGAINST candidates who stand for an issue or way of life they reject.

73. Research campaign issues personally if you possibly can; you must be credible on the issues.

74. Pick two or three major issues and stick with them; learn them frontward and backward and upside down.

75. Avoid getting side-tracked into debating issues unrelated to your office.

76. Carefully investigate tips about unethical or illegal activities by your opponent and handle them like a time bomb.

Tips 77-81: OPPONENTS

77. Keep your strongest opponents out of the race by any means possible within ethical and legal constraints.

78. Understand that running against a "bad guy" is easier and more rewarding than against one who is perceived as a "nice guy."

79. Avoid falling for the "ladies first" ploy; it is not to your advantage on the speaker's platform with your opponent.

80. Don't be discouraged by what you hear or read in the newspapers about how well your opponent is doing; it's often wishful thinking or creative advertising.

81. Refute an opponent's charge publicly if people will assume you are acquiescing to the merits of the issue without response.

Tips 82-85: MEDIA

82. Have your scheduler contact every editor who will make endorsements in your race immediately after filing deadline to schedule an endorsement interview.

83. Seek unusual ways to get air time and press coverage.

84. Keep yourself informed of media coverage in your race, both news and editorial, everywhere in your district.

85. Decide in advance exactly where you want to be when the earliest election returns are broadcast.

Tips 86-94: CANDIDATE PERSONAL MATTERS

86. Expect severe disruption of your family life.

87. Anticipate enormous curiosity about your relationship with your spouse or partner.

88. Reach an up-front understanding of what involvement your family will commit to the campaign to save tempers and staff misunderstandings later.

89. Find a part-time housekeeper before the campaign crunch hits.

90. Consider getting an unlisted home phone number and install an answering machine.

91. Upgrade your wardrobe and consider it a hidden, but unavoidable, personal campaign cost.

92. Get professional advice about your haircut and glasses early in the campaign.

93. Live your personal life as if the details will show up in the morning paper.

94. Have a contingency plan for what you will do professionally if you lose the election, even if you don't tell another soul about it.

Tips 95-101: EVERYTHING ELSE

95. Know you will be criticized; it is an unavoidable and unending rite of passage to seeking and serving in public office.

96. Expect some erosion and defection from your support base, occasionally by individuals you counted on as friends.

97. Learn to take the peaks and valleys in stride; campaigns are teeter-totters with abrupt ups and downs.

98. Keep going: Persevere, one step at a time, each day at a time, doing what you can, even when the odds don't look promising.

99. View yourself as a lightbulb everyone else needs to touch for energy and recharging.

100. Get out of politics if running for office ceases to be fun. On the other hand, if you're undeterred by the preceding cautions, GO FOR IT. You are needed!

101. Invite everyone to attend your election night celebration. Make election night your finest hour, regardless of what has happened during the race.

INTRODUCTION

*"There will be a lot of little girls who open their history texts to
see my picture ...and they will say, 'If she can do it, so can I.'"*

--Texas Governor Ann Richards,
November, 1990

Greater opportunities than ever before beckon women to seek elective office.

Voters perceive women as possessing special attributes for the political arena: strong communication skills in speaking, listening and writing; patience; less ego-driven agendas than male politicians; willingness to compromise versus a "win-at-all-costs" approach; ability to relate to individual voters and instill confidence in government; trustworthiness; not being as likely as men to succumb to corruption.

On the other hand, women candidates need to be better organized than men, overcome confining stereotypes, work harder to raise money, avoid seeming too ambitious, pay more attention to issues, find early male endorsers to help establish credibility, be more careful about using negative campaign tactics, conquer lack of self-confidence, more effectively delegate responsibilities, more carefully clarify expectations with their campaign managers, give more thought to how their family relationships will be viewed by others, get used to adulation and being waited upon, and be prepared for labels such as "shrill," "bitchy" and "sweet."

On top of it all, they have to lighten up, smile more, and learn not to take it too personally—to have fun with it and enjoy the challenge—because politics is, after all, a game of chance and skill.

None of these prerequisites is unique to politics. Women seeking managerial and leadership roles in any field encounter similar challenges. Women entrepreneurs searching for capital loans must justify their case more thoroughly than men, a corollary to the struggle female candidates experience in raising money for their campaigns.

Women in the private sector make career decisions later in life, just as most female candidates are older than male candidates when they enter public life. In 1987, the average age of men new to Congress was 45; for women it was 54. This nine-year lag places women at a disadvantage in building seniority and long-term records of accomplishment. Nevertheless, the public benefits from their maturity and depth of experience.

Only 21% of men wait until ages 40 through 59 to launch a state legislative career, while 61% of women begin during those ages. A 1981 study by the Center for the American Woman and Politics (CAWP) at Rutgers University found that the factors which most influenced women's decisions to run were: "Having a loyal group of friends and supporters behind me," "Realization that I was just as capable of holding office as most officeholders," "Belief that I was strong enough to combat any discrimination I might encounter," "Knowing that my children were old enough that I would not be needed at home as much," and "Support of my spouse."

The second pattern of difference between men and women managers noted by Drs. Margaret Hennig and Anne Jardim in *The Managerial Woman* was a sense of passivity which is paralleled by the lack of ambition traditionally exhibited by women in the political realm.

The third point of departure was the overwhelming sense of "waiting to be chosen" by women, a nearly-universal trait. Too many women sit on the bench until they're invited to dance; waiting to be solicited to serve on the school board or as president of the state assessors' association. The feminist movement is helping to alter this attitude, but it is still a tendency women need to overcome.

The concept of power—how and when and why to wield it—is a related issue not yet adequately explored. What is difficult to acquire is "a comfort level with power itself," as former Vermont Governor Madeline Kunin told an audience at the Kennedy School of Government at Harvard University in October 1989. "It is not lack of polling data or campaign contributions which keeps many women from ascending higher on the political ladder," Kunin said, "it is fear and loathing of the political system itself. But while many men may be equally repelled by the political practices of our time, they are better equipped to deal with them. The public is also accustomed to seeing boys fight. In fact, they relish it. Girls are still not supposed to . . . ."

Gains by women in politics have been gradual but steady over the past twenty years. The number of women serving in state legislatures has increased by about one percent nationally every election cycle. Still, only 17% of those who serve in our elected legislative and governing bodies are female. Women comprise barely 6% of our nation's Congress. The higher the level of decision-making, the smaller the percentage of women serving in elected positions.

All three states which elected women as governors in 1990—Texas, Kansas, Oregon—had previously elected women to highly-visible offices.

Women mayors had served in seven of the ten largest cities in Texas and Governor Richards herself had earned accolades as State Treasurer. Kansas had been represented in the nation's capital for twelve years by Senator Nancy Kassebaum and for six years by Representative Jan Meyers before the voters elected Joan Finney as governor.

In Oregon, both Betty Roberts (a Democrat, no relation to Barbara Roberts, the current governor) and Norma Paulus, a Republican, had previously run credible gubernatorial races. Paulus had served for eight years as Secretary of State before her gubernatorial campaign, and Barbara Roberts for six years as Secretary of State. In Barbara Roberts' 1990 campaign for governor, gender was not a major issue.

This book presents an overview, from the candidate's point of view, of what is required *before* and *during* a woman's campaign for public office. It does not replace the need for a campaign manual for campaign workers. Sample forms, check-off lists and detailed guidelines will still be needed.

Six questions can be used to analyze the viability of a campaign:

1) How tough is (are) the opponent(s)? Is our candidate in the right race at the right time?

2) How well organized is our candidate? Does she have a campaign plan? Campaign manager? Prior campaign experience? Prior civic and leadership experience?

3) Are her fund-raising plan and budget adequate and reasonable? Will she raise the money?

4) Who is helping and advising her?

5) Does she have two strong issues to run on?

6) How hard is she willing to work? Is she healthy, energetic, enthusiastic, caring? How realistic is her understanding of what is required to win?

Throughout this book, advice concerning questions like these is interwoven into the 101 tips for women candidates and their staffs. Races for statewide and congressional offices require a more complex organization than those for lower-visibility offices, and the reader will need to keep those differences in mind while reading this book.

If you are considering running for a volunteer position in your local community, don't be overwhelmed or scared off by the tips which apply only to larger races. It would be overkill, for example, to hire paid staff when seeking a local hospital or lighting board position. Service district elections usually involve little more than the cost of a filing fee. Because this book aims to be as inclusive as possible, all tips won't apply in every race.

The bigger the campaign, the more a candidate's efforts must be devoted solely to fund raising and media exposure. The candidate and her family are much more likely to be personally involved in the day-to-day details of running a small campaign than in a larger one.

In spite of such variations, most of these 101 campaign tips apply in some degree to every candidate. Each jurisdiction also has its own election and reporting laws which must be complied with, as noted in various parts of this book. Several tips contain reference to restrictions in judicial races and include special advice for women candidates for judgeships.

The National Women's Political Caucus calls the '90s the "Decade for Women in Politics." The 1990 census forced the realignment of Congressional and legislative district lines based on population shifts, to be effective in 1992. A flurry of term limitation measures (approved in 1990 for California, Colorado, and Oklahoma) may create "musical chairs" scenarios throughout the political system which will open even more opportunities for female candidates.

"Women of every political stripe...are letting down their own sexual side by not demanding more female candidates and by not supporting them when they run...," *New York Times* columnist William Safire said recently. "Not enough women are candidates, and too few of those are winning. Why? The power of incumbency is an excuse, as is the tug of tradition and the demands of rearing children. The reason, however, is a dismaying lack of assertiveness of group identity....Other things being roughly equal, women should strongly support women as women until some parity is reached. Then, secure in a system in balance, they can throw the rascals out regardless of sex."

Women still fare best in contests for open seats. National women's groups and both political parties will be recruiting volunteers for these races. The best candidates, however, will be those who are self-motivated, who have, perhaps without realizing it, already started preparing to someday seek public office. A campaign presents an exciting challenge, a stimulating adventure, a peak life experience. Even losing candidates acknowledge the valuable education gained in seeking public office.

In order for more women to be elected, more women must run. Perhaps you will be one of them. If not, surely you know someone you can help persuade to take this worthwhile journey.

TIPS 1 - 18
The Decision To Run

1

Visualize yourself in the role of candidate for months, even years, before you run. Imagine yourself as an elected official who shakes hands with her constituents, responds to reporters' questions, champions important causes. Dreams can come true.

Start small. Make your vision something which stretches you, but not outrageously. Join a civic organization, seek an appointment to a board or commission, take action on a community issue you care about. If you're a homemaker who has never chaired a meeting, running for Congress would be unrealistic. You could do it in the long haul, step-by-step—perhaps starting as president of your local League of Women Voters or chairing your county planning commission, next running for the state legislature, then tackling Congress.

Researchers in the field of peak performance have found that you reach your highest achievement when you begin with a goal in mind. People who see themselves, hear themselves, feel themselves running, winning, succeeding, are most apt to do so. It's called visualization. Success literature available in your libraries and bookstores—books, tapes, videos—contains valuable self-help tools on this topic.

Daydreams are healthy; they possess enormous power, psychologically and physiologically, for directing your life. All things are created twice—first mentally, then in reality, says Stephen Covey in *The Seven Habits of Highly Effective People*. Think of a woman role model. Imagine yourself as you picture her.

Taking an active role in your community—in your local schools, churches, synagogues, library boards, museums, citizens' advisory committees, political parties. Look for activities that will help you meet potential voters, gain visibility, and acquire support bases.

Also consider whether your voting address and political party affiliation are to your advantage. Independents seldom get elected except in non-partisan races. Consider moving to another street or district if your party affiliation hampers your election chances where you presently live, or change parties if your party no longer fits your ideas. Many people register initially without giving the matter much thought. Both major parties represent such a wide range of political philosophies that many people could fit under either banner in most parts of the country.

Positioning yourself for the possibility of a future race, even if you never do it, keeps you flexible and available to act quickly if the right opportunity comes. The more you develop leadership and learn assertiveness, the more convincing you will be when and if the campaign spotlight shines on you.

2 *Find a political mentor.* Working on a campaign as a volunteer or paid staff member is an ideal way to get started in politics. Talk to women officials in your area whom you admire, and seek their backing. Hire on as a staff member to an elected official.

A respected public official who takes you under his or her wing can teach you the ropes and lend you credibility. Such a mentor can also act as a role model, providing on-the-job training to learn politics up close, day after day.

"Women and their managers fight throughout their campaigns to establish their qualifications, power, toughness, and capacity to win—traits assumed . . . to be inherent in most male candidates," a report prepared in 1989 for EMILY's List by Greenburg-Lake said. One method suggested for overcoming this credibility gap was for female candidates to gain early endorsements, especially well-known and respected male office holders.

Nancy Kassebaum started her public service on a small-town school board before following the political legacy of her father,* 1936 Republican presidential nominee Alf Landon. California Congresswoman Nancy Pelosi also learned politics from her father, a former mayor of Baltimore, and Congresswoman Liz Patterson is the daughter of a former U.S. senator and governor of South Carolina. Congresswoman Barbara Vucanovich served as a district representative for former Senator Paul Laxalt and was active in Republican party politics before winning Nevada's new U.S. House seat in 1982.

---

* Upon her election to the U.S. Senate in 1978, Kassebaum became the first woman in U.S. history elected senator who had not followed her husband into politics, according to *Women Leaders in Contemporary U.S. Politics*, by Frank LeVeness and Jane Sweeney. In May 1991, Republican Kassebaum was pictured on the cover of *Time* magazine along with four men as possible future U.S. vice-presidential candidate suggestions for George Bush. In the 102nd Congress of 1991-92, Kassebaum and Democrat Barbara Mikulski of Maryland were the only two women U.S. Senators out of a hundred—a 2% female representation.

California Treasurer Kathleen Brown follows in the political tradition of two former California governors—her father "Pat" Brown (1959-66) and brother Jerry Brown (1975-82.) She toured the state as part of her father's entourage while in grade school (although harboring no such aspirations for herself), was elected to the Los Angeles Board of Education in 1974, and was viewed as an up-and-coming political star as soon as she announced for state treasurer in 1989. "Telegenic and comfortable in front of a camera," *Business Week* said of her. Columnist David S. Broder said before Brown took office, "California will finally have a statewide Democratic official with the potential to be on the national ticket."

Most elected officials are generous in their willingness to advise and assist the campaigns of others. They will be especially grateful to someone who has contributed time and energy to their own election efforts. But don't expect others to read your mind; make your ambitions known early so they can help you keep an eye out for possible opportunities.

3 *Assess your strengths and weaknesses for becoming a candidate.* **Make a list of your strong qualities and drawbacks for seeking office. Don't be modest; most women grievously underestimate their capabilities. Analyze your financial, mental, physical, and marital health; evaluate your name familiarity, financial backing, volunteer forces, family support, knowledge of issues, commitment to public service, appearance, strength of ego, and willingness to throw yourself head first into a grueling campaign.**

Be brutally honest about your chances of success, remembering that *nobody is the perfect candidate.* **Keep in mind that skills needed to get elected may differ markedly from those required once you are in office.**

Try the following quiz to see how you would rate yourself. Then ask a couple of candid friends to score you. Be sure your own perceptions and theirs aren't too far apart.

Don't assume that a low score on any question would automatically disqualify you. It might mean, however, that you need to defuse or downplay a potential negative.

RATE YOURSELF AS A POTENTIAL CANDIDATE

(Scale 1 - 10; 10 for a strong "yes")

ASK YOUR FRIENDS TO RATE YOU!

A. Appearance and Intangible Personal Assets:

___ 1. Do you have a good sense of humor?

___ 2. Are you healthy and energetic; do you have stamina?

___ 3. Do you like meeting new people?

___ 4. Are you persistent and hard-working?

___ 5. Do you have an engaging smile?

___ 6. Are you viewed as honest, sincere, trust-worthy?

___ 7. Is your physical appearance attractive? Are you neat and well-groomed?

___ 8. Are your self-confident? Can you "sell" yourself?

___ 9. Do you have tested leadership skills, including experience in delegating? Are you decisive, able to say no?

___ 10. How tough are you? Do you have a thick skin or could you develop one? *(Subtract 10 points if you cry at the drop of a hat.)*

___ 11. Are you a practiced public speaker and/or able to articulate ideas well?

___ 12. Do you have a simple, memorable name?

___ 13. Are you well-organized?

___ 14. Do you like participating in group sports such as volleyball and softball or other team contests?

___ 15. Do you enjoy playing poker, bridge, or other games which test strategy skills and willingness to take risks?

___ 16. Are you smart, intuitive, a quick study?

___ 17. Would your hair style appeal to people who have never met you and would base their voting decision solely on your picture? (If not, would you be willing to modify it?)

___ 18. Could you afford to buy a few new clothes and get your hair styled?

___ 19. Are you well-informed about the area where you live and do you stay abreast of local news?

___ 20. Do you have name familiarity in all parts of your district?

___ 21. Are you flexible?

___ 22. Have you worked on other political campaigns, led charitable fund-raising drives, or started your own business?

___ 23. If previously a candidate for public office or a manager for a contested race, how successful were you?

___ 24. Are you free of personal habits or traits which voters might find distasteful, such as gum chewing, nail biting, smoking, sloppiness, heavy use of perfume, overindulging in food or drink, use of offensive language?

___ 25. Do you have a history of love affairs, excessive drinking, or drug use, etc. which could hurt your candidacy? (Assume all skeletons *will be* exposed.)

B. Family Finances, and Friends:

___ 26. If married or committed, is that relationship stable and supportive? *(If single, score 5 points.)*

___ 27. Are your family's finances in good order?

___ 28. Could your family survive without you during the campaign? *(If not applicable, score 5 points.)*

___ 29. Do you have friends who would contribute their time, money, and energy to help get you elected?

___ 30. Are you involved in community organizations, especially ones with members who would support your candidacy?

___ 31. Do you understand public budgets and taxes?

___ 32. Are there issues you could run on which have advocates who would work for your election?

___ 33 Could your work survive without you during the campaign? *(If not applicable, score 5 points.)*

___ 34. Would members of your family hit the campaign trail and ask their friends and colleagues to contribute money?

___ 35. Are the closets of your family members and close business associates free from skeletons which could hurt your candidacy?

C. Campaign Readiness:

___ 36. Are there public issues you care deeply about?

___ 37. Could you do a better job than the incumbent who represents you in the state legislature, city or county commission, school board, or other elected office?

___ 38. To what degree is good government important to you?

___ 39. Do you have issues of shared concern with the voters in your district; are you in tune with your constituents?

___ 40. Are you willing to listen with respect to the opinions of others?

___ 41. Would you consider altering your positions based on valid new information?

___ 42. Have you "paid your dues" in service to your political party (if this is important in your area)?

___ 43. Are you willing to promote yourself as a candidate before audiences, on the phone, and possibly (depending on the office sought) door-to-door? *(Subtract 10 points for a score of 2 or less.)*

___ 44. Could you devote eighty hours a week to campaigning if need be? *(If contemplating a hotly contested race, subtract 10 points for a score of 2 or less.)*

___ 45. Do you want this job so badly you can feel it in your teeth? *(Subtract 5 points for a score of 2 or less.)*

(See scale of ratings next page)

RATINGS:

    Over 400: **Run for U.S. President! Your country needs you.**

    251-400: **Start planning your local or state campaign.**

    200-250: **Work to improve your rating, reevaluate in two years.**

  Under 200: **Help your favorite candidate get elected.**

4

> *Be sure you have the "fire in your belly" to run.* You need a firm resolve, an ability to work hard, and a willingness to heed the advice of others more experienced than you. This zeal may come from issues you care strongly about, broad goals for good government, or the simple desire to serve in elective office.

Coaxing by others won't give you the perseverance needed in down times. The *commitment*, the *drive*, the *ambition*, must come from within. If it doesn't, you will be overwhelmed by the burdens of campaigning and begrudge the 15-hour days and 7-day weeks which may be required. You will wonder bitterly where all the people are who were so anxious to see you run.

As more groups actively recruit female candidates, the line between feeling flattered because you were asked and inner drive becomes especially important. Women need to be sought out, encouraged, and coached in the techniques of campaigning, but "being asked" should not be a major consideration. Recruiting should make women aware that opportunities* not previously available are now open and reassure them that they have the attributes of a successful candidate.

When Washington Congresswoman Jolene Unsoeld was recruited as a congressional candidate by the Women's Campaign Fund and EMILY's List in 1988, Unsoeld was serving in the state legislature and thought she was too old, at 56, to be changing political careers. The recruiters helped Unsoeld overcome her doubts, pointing out that Louisiana's Lindy Boggs and others had begun their Washington D.C. elective service at the same age or older.

For example, Republican Congresswoman Helen Delich Bentley of Maryland was first elected to Congress in 1984 at the age of 61, unseating a 22-year incumbent. Prior to her congressional career, Bentley worked as a reporter and maritime editor for the Baltimore *Sun* for 24 years, and served for six years as Chair of the Federal Maritime Commission.**

---

* The study of political ambition was pioneered by political scientist Joseph A. Schlesinger (*Ambition and Politics*, 1966.) Later researchers have found that political ambition develops slowly in response to perceived opportunities and changing circumstances.

** Biographical information regarding Helen Delich Bentley and other women in Congress was obtained from the *1989 National Directory of Women Elected Officials* published by the National Women's Political Caucus.

You can't be shy and modest as a candidate. The nature of politics requires selling yourself and enjoying working with other people. If you assume campaign duties reluctantly as a first-time candidate, you'd be better off to spend your energies helping recruit and elect other women.

"Generally, the less agonizing the decision-making process, the better suited you are to run," says political consultant Cathy Allen. If you have to think about it too long and hard, you probably aren't the best candidate.

However, don't expect everyone to applaud your ambition. Here's what the *Reno Gazette-Journal* said in its endorsement of 41-year-old Secretary of State Frankie Sue Del Papa's successful candidacy for Nevada Attorney General in 1990: "The combination of a strong record of government and administrative responsibilities with legal experience makes her the strongest candidate for the position....One note of concern, though: Throughout her political career, Del Papa has appeared to be overly committed to fast-track advancement. There is nothing wrong with setting career goals nor raw ambition. But if elected, the voters of this state have the right to expect her to distinguish herself as attorney general before committing to her next career step."

A refreshing change, a woman with visible political ambition! (Del Papa laid the groundwork for her A.G. position by serving as an assistant to two U. S. Senators and clerking for a federal judge.)

5 *Seek an office with no incumbent to increase your odds of winning.* **No other campaign asset matches the formidable power of incumbency. Toppling a current office holder can be done, but it takes the right candidate, a vulnerable opponent, the right timing, and adequate resources.**

Eighty-three percent of incumbents are male—and most incumbents get reelected. The return rate for members of Congress was 96% in 1990, down only 2% from 98% in 1988.

Incumbents are difficult to unseat for many reasons: financial war chests, name familiarity, bulk mailing privileges paid for with taxpayer money, loyal staff members who take leave to run their campaigns, availability of speaker's forums and extensive computer files of names and addresses and targeting information. Constituent service which members of Congress perform every day closely resembles campaign activity in its outreach to individual voters. Furthermore, the strongest candidates seldom challenge incumbents. The political maxim is: "You can't beat a horse without a horse."

Statistics gathered by Common Cause show that House incumbents raised nearly 13 times as much money from PACs as did challengers in 1990. Only one woman, Congresswoman Jolene Unsoeld of Washington State, was on the list of 15 U.S. Senators and Representatives who were the top recipients of 1990 PAC contributions. Of the 345 women who challenged incumbent members of Congress during the twenty years 1970 through 1990, only 11, or 3% won.*

The myth of invulnerable incumbents has become a self-fulfilling prophecy, says the sole woman to unseat an incumbent member of Congress in 1990—Joan Kelly Horn of Missouri. Outspent two-to-one, Horn parlayed her knowledge of political strategy and campaign techniques to a squeaky 54-vote victory. (She and her husband ran their own political consulting firm for fifteen years prior to Horn's successful bid for office.)

In one of the biggest surprises of the 1990 fall elections, a political newcomer named Christine Todd Whitman came within four percentage points of beating incumbent U.S. Senator Bill Bradley of New Jersey, who had been boosted as a future presidential candidate. The media blamed Bradley's failure to take a position on an unpopular state tax increase for his narrow loss, but Whitman, a former Board of Public Utilities President, made her strong showing on a war chest a fraction of the size of Bradley's ($670,000 to $12,300,000).

With only 2 percent name familiarity at the beginning of her race, Congresswoman Nita Lowey of New York unseated an incumbent—the only woman congressional candidate in 1988 to do so. Lowey turned the potential negative of never having held elective office to a positive attribute by billing herself as "the experienced Democrat." Since neither of her primary rivals had government experience, her use of prior service in the Secretary of State's office was effective. (She also peppered the airwaves and mails with advertising to get her name known, and was paired in the general election against an incumbent plagued by a scandal.)

In 1990, challenger Rosemary Mulligan won the Republican nomination for an Illinois house seat by a coin toss to break a tie vote,

---

* Seventy-nine women sought *open* congressional seats from 1970 through 1990, of which 33, or 42%, won their races. This data and many other statistics in this book were taken from fact sheets prepared by the Center for the American Woman and Politics (CAWP), National Information Bank of Women in Public Office, Eagleton Institute of Politics, Rutgers University.

only to have that victory overturned by the Illinois Supreme Court six weeks before the general election. Running as a political unknown in the Chicago suburbs of Park Ridge and Des Plains, Mulligan used her solid Business and Professional Women (BPW) base to launch her campaign. She used accountability and the incumbent's record as her platform—the first time the 14-year incumbent had faced a serious primary challenge. Mulligan immediately made plans to run again in 1992 against the same incumbent.

An army of volunteers walked the streets in Ada County (Boise), Idaho, in 1990 to help Sally Snodgrass oust a three-term state senator who had recently been elected majority leader. In a heavily Republican district, Democrat Snodgrass took her campaign to the people. While she was motivated to run by her pro-choice views, that was not a big issue in the race. A large number of voters felt disenfranchised by the incumbent, whom Snodgrass described as an arrogant man with "almost a stone demeanor." He had never before had to campaign hard and didn't take her seriously until two or three weeks before the election. On a $30,000 budget, Snodgrass won by 300 votes, 51% to 49%.

"Getting Back to the Mainstream" was the theme of Republican Connie Wible's successful 1990 campaign for a seat in the Missouri House of Representatives. "I will represent all the people and not just a few," she told the voters. The incumbent, a first-term Republican woman with a charismatic personality and extreme right-wing views, was outspent and outworked by Wible and a crew of enthusiastic volunteers on the campaign trail. Wible won with an 11-point edge and captured the seat handily in the fall.

Sometimes you have to run against an incumbent. If he or she is out of step with your district, the current office-holder may be vulnerable. An advantage to taking on an incumbent is that you usually have the field to yourself instead of facing a dozen eager contestants as in the scramble for an open seat. Another advantage may be that the incumbent has enemies who would provide some support to a challenger. Even so, your best chance of getting elected is to run for an open seat.

6

Become a proven vote getter to position yourself as a viable candidate for higher office. You are credible and "viable" to the degree that people believe you can win. Votes previously cast at the ballot box are proof of electability. Many full-time elected officials began their political careers far down the political ladder.

The strongest predictor of success for women candidates is experience in elective office, according to a nationwide study of women candidates conducted by Susan J. Carroll in 1976 as reported in *Women as Candidates in American Politics.*

No matter what level position you hold, an elective office title will help you establish credibility with potential contributors and the public. People like to see a candidate on her way up and will contribute time and energy based on future promise.

Congresswoman Maxine Waters of California developed her fire-eater image in the state legislature while she eyed a congressional seat for nearly a decade. A dynamo of energy and drive, Waters built a solid record of accomplishment as an elected official and let it be widely known that the 29th Congressional District was hers when the incumbent stepped down—and in 1990 it was.*

Illinois elected its first woman statewide governmental official, Dawn Clark Netsch, in 1990. State Controller Netsch had previously served several terms in the State Senate. As Virginia's Attorney General, Mary Sue Terry is getting name exposure to position herself for a future gubernatorial bid. Republican Congresswoman Marge Roukema of New Jersey, a secondary school teacher, was first elected to the Ridgewood Board of Education in 1970. An active leader in community issues, she lost her first bid for Congress in 1978, but two years later unseated a three-term incumbent.

A year after Controller Kathy Whitmire was elected as Houston's first female officeholder, nearly one-third of voters surveyed said their attitudes had changed positively as a result of her performance. She was later elected mayor of Houston, the nation's fourth-largest city.

---

* Congresswoman Waters joined three other black Congresswomen: Cardiss Collins of Illinois, an 18-year veteran of the House; newly-elected Barbara-Rose Collins of Michigan, a former Detroit City Council member; and Eleanor Holmes Norton, new non-voting delegate from Washington, D.C., former chair of the Equal Employment Opportunity Commission.

Elective office can also serve as a stepping stone to high appointive office. Illinois Congresswoman Lynn Martin, who lost her 1990 U.S. Senate bid, gained an appointment as Secretary of Labor. After Massachusetts Congresswoman Margaret Heckler lost her reapportioned district in 1982, she went on to serve as Secretary of Health and Human Services. Sandra Day O'Connor was reelected twice as a state senator (after first being appointed to serve), then elected County Superior Court Judge before being appointed to the Arizona Court of Appeals. In 1981, she made history as the first woman appointed to the U.S. Supreme Court.

Well-known Republican women who achieved high appointive positions in government without first serving in elective positions include Transportation Secretary Elizabeth Dole, Ambassador to the United Nations Jeane Kirkpatrick, and U.S. Civil Rights Commission Officer Jill Ruckelshaus.*

7 *Be in top physical condition before embarking upon a campaign.* **Expect a different kind of exhaustion than you've ever experienced—caused by lack of sleep, insomnia, emotional stress, irregular schedules, constant pressure, and no time off. You may also be affected by rich foods, second-hand smoke, second-hand perfume, little or no exercise (except in races utilizing door-to-door strategy) and the temptation to relieve the stress with too much alcohol. The need for physical stamina is seldom given adequate credence by first-time candidates and staff.**

Nothing energizes campaign workers more than their candidate's energy, enthusiasm and drive. Good health is the basic ingredient; it shows when you don't feel up to par. There's no leeway for getting sick or keeping dentist's appointments once the campaign goes into high gear.

Have complete physical and dental checkups before beginning a campaign. Buy comfortable walking shoes and break them in ahead of time. Maintain some exercise routine, if only ten minutes a day in your room. Drink plain soda water at events and remember that no one likes seeing a candidate with her hands and mouth full of food.

Candidates who canvass door-to-door need abundant physical and mental stamina to pound the sidewalk or asphalt for hours on end, day

---

* Jill Ruckelshaus authored the memorable line: "No one should have to dance backward all their lives!"

after day, two to six months before the election. With two pairs of comfortable walking shoes, you can change on alternate days to give your feet a rest. Shun high heels. Fancy shoes won't bring you votes; a smile on your face will.

If you smoke, reduce your habit to a few cigarettes a day and carefully choose where and when you light up. Better yet—give it up completely.

The same goes for alcohol. Either avoid it altogether or limit your intake to a glass or two of wine a day, preferably at home. None is best; it keeps your mind clear, your speech coherent, and you awake. Your supporters will be embarrassed and ill-at-ease if you overindulge.

Candidates who are recovering alcoholics or have a past drinking problem should air that issue early in the campaign, and thus diffuse it. In County Commissioner Gretchen Kafoury's 1990 race for Portland (Oregon) City Council, she polled voters to ask how they would feel if they learned she had overcome a problem with alcoholism. The campaign then deliberately leaked this poll question to the press four months before Kafoury announced her successful candidacy, co-opting negative use of that information by her opponent.

8

Activate your campaign nine months to a year before a primary. **Even two years ahead is not too early to commence internal planning, nor is ten years too soon to start positioning yourself for a future race. But keep flexible. Be ready to move when vacancies occur or other opportunities arise.**

The earlier a candidate makes the decision to run, the more likely she is to win her race. Susan Carroll's study found a positive correlation between how early a woman decided to run and the winning of her primary election.

As in any other business, the more advance planning and preparation you do for your campaign ahead of time, the greater its chance of success.

Once you've made up your mind, keep the news under your hat until a few essentials are in place. A campaign treasurer must be designated, an interim campaign address decided upon, a quiet work space found where things can be left undisturbed at night—your extra bedroom—your campaign manager's basement—an unused office cubicle at someone's place of business.

Most importantly, you need someone helping you—a paid consultant, your new campaign manager, an experienced volunteer—before you make your formal announcement. Your announcement of candidacy may be your best shot at free publicity during the entire campaign, so don't waste it. Have a good photograph ready and a written statement covering your campaign high points: budget, issues, campaign treasurer, motivation for running, and especially important if challenging an incumbent, why you expect to win. Call a press conference and invite all radio, TV and press contacts in your area.

9

Know the office you're aspiring to and the election laws governing your race. **Opportunities to learn can come from interviews with present and previous holders of the position, office employees, proposed and adopted budgets, audits, publications, public meetings and newspaper articles.**

"Politics is perhaps the only profession for which no preparation is thought necessary," said poet Robert Louis Stevenson over a century ago. Some people still subscribe to that theory. Smart candidates do not.

Qualifications can give a woman candidate the self-confidence and credibility she needs to mount a viable campaign. However, qualifications won't be enough to win a race for you at the ballot box. "Qualifications appear to have little effect on election outcomes," researcher Susan Carroll found. "It is not the case that those who are more qualified win while those who lack qualifications lose."

A major hurdle women must overcome is self-doubt about their competence; having strong qualifications helps instill self-confidence. In addition, knowing about the office you seek and understanding the issues of your district will give you assurance. If you can articulate ideas for needed changes, you're headed in the right direction.

Study local and state election laws regarding residency and other requirements for your area. Find out what forms must be filed and when. Accounting and reporting laws are particularly important; a candidate can quickly get into trouble here. Most states have specific regulations covering the acceptance of campaign contributions. In many states, it is illegal to accept money before you have filed a formal statement of intent or organization and/or designated a political treasurer.

10

Consider touching base with your hometown editor before making a final commitment to enter a major race. **Find out the newspaper protocol in your community. For legislative and less visible races, you may wish to put this off until after you have filed.**

In any case, wait until you can articulate your plans for accomplishment in office and why you want to run before you talk to any editors. Two months before the election, ask two or three supporters whose opinions the editors respect to phone them and urge your endorsement.

If you presently hold office, it's good political strategy to call newspaper editors who have previously endorsed you to find out how they feel about your performance in office. Tell them about your future political alternatives and get a reality check from their reactions. They may also give you added insights about up-coming issues.

Editors make dozens of endorsement decisions, usually before the battle lines in a campaign are clearly drawn. They solicit feedback from reporters and columnists who cover political beats, and sometimes do reference checks on candidates. Like anyone else, editors respect the opinions of trusted friends and acquaintances, which is why it is worthwhile to find a respected community leader to put in a good word for you at endorsement time.

Most newspapers expect you to contact them for an appointment, rather than waiting for the newspaper to seek you out. *The burden is on you to call six to eight weeks before the election to present your case for endorsement.*

11

Contact friends, acquaintances, prominent persons, and potential contributors for support and advice before you declare. In seeking opinions before announcing your candidacy, you offer people a stake in your enterprise. Even those who make no promises will often stay neutral or come around later because you approached them personally. Give folks a reason to tell your opponents, "Sorry, Joan asked me first."

It's like the game of Monopoly—the goal is to accumulate all the territory you can. Then wherever your opponents try to land, they will find you've already staked out a claim.

First-time candidates can get out-hustled before they realize what's going on. Start making lists of all kinds of people to contact. It's particularly important to move fast if you and your potential opponent(s) have friends and acquaintances in common. The race will be uncomfortable for mutual friends and acquaintances and the early bird candidate can neutralize her opponent's chances.

Seek the advice of friends, acquaintances and political insiders before you announce publicly. Ask what they think your biggest strengths and weaknesses are as a candidate and ask for their support—endorsements, dollars, services.

Don't be intimidated by the thought of raising money. If you've never solicited contributions, the idea can be overwhelming. But people like you learn to do it every day; it's a skill that can be acquired.

Don't forget to make courtesy calls to your mentors and other elected officials. In partisan races, you may want to restrict your calls to members of your own political party. Guessing who's going to run for what race is part of the fun of politics. Everyone likes to be the first to know, especially about races in their home territory. Ask the advice of other elected officials, but check with your advisors before following it.

12

Consider withdrawing before filing deadline to keep your name off the ballot if your chances of making a decent showing are nil. Occasionally a candidate should withdraw to save her best shot for another race. Once your name is on the ballot, a loss can't be erased from your record. Then the only way you can avoid losing is to win. Make your decision before the last minute to avoid the appearance of indecisiveness or that you lack the nerve to run.

If you've already announced your candidacy, lined up support and collected money, your credibility is at stake if you withdraw from a race. You and your advisors must decide whether it is best in the long-run to withdraw as quietly as possible or to use up your supporters' good will in facing a rout. A first-time batter in politics gets only one wild strike and she's out. You're not likely to get (or want) a second chance if you fail miserably.

On the other hand, the opportunity for name exposure could keep a candidate in a race even when she expects to lose. Possible benefits include increased name familiarity and building of a support base for a future race, raising significant issues which need to be aired, the opportunity to meet new people, a free education in political science, and personal gains such as bringing in customers to your insurance business, accounting office or delicatessen. Small-town lawyers are sometimes advised to run for office to become better known in the community.

If you run an organized campaign and make a respectable showing, you will have earned visibility and respect. But if your chances are hopeless, consider withdrawing before filing deadline to wait for a better day. Losing may build character and teach humility, but it's hard to think of anything else good to say about it. The blow to your ego of losing a race may be harsher than you think. If you're a first-time candidate who entered the race late and then got hit with unexpectedly powerful opposition, consider saving your best effort for another match.

13

Don't assume that organizations you belong to or whose principles you espouse will automatically support you. Unless you have received personal assurances from key leaders that you can count on that organization's endorsement, you are naive to expect it. Membership in an association guarantees nothing, nor does previous support of that group's issues—unless you have played a major and publicly-visible role championing their cause.

Organizations and political action committees (PACs) support candidates for a wide variety of reasons, but they generally want to pick a winner. It's like placing bets at the race track. If you are running against an incumbent, people and groups may find it hard to back a newcomer because they fear the wrath of the incumbent if he or she is reelected.

Some PACs support only a limited number of candidates so they won't spread their resources too thin, in which case you will compete with candidates for other offices as well as your own opponent. A few groups contribute only in specialized races and others won't endorse you unless you agree 100% with their detailed agendas.

As a first-time candidate, you may find the going tough because political insiders don't know enough about you; you're an unknown quantity. People are more comfortable with someone they can predict than a political unknown. It's a Catch-22: You can't get elected without experience, and you can't get experience without being elected.

When two viable, pro-choice women run against each other, many women's groups will make joint endorsements or stay out of the race entirely if both candidates seek their support. But if necessary to keep a third candidate from winning, the stronger of the two endorsable female candidates may be supported.

Note the phrase above, "if both candidates seek their support." Many organizations will ignore you completely if you don't seek them out. Think of yourself as an entrepreneur and the organizations as potential clients; they're not going to come to you, you have to go after them.

14

Don't underestimate the effect of your candidacy on your co-workers, clients, employees, and friends. Whether you are in the public or private sector, everything you say or do will be judged differently once you become a candidate. Expect some negative fallout on your business and work atmosphere. Friends may decide you are not the person they thought because you are willing to be a "politician." Be prepared to deal with the negative connotations of that word.

"Public office is the last refuge of a scoundrel," said a *Colliers Weekly* squib in 1931. Sixty years later, politicians still strive to overcome this perception. Women have an advantage here because voters perceive them as less susceptible to corruption, more caring about individuals, less caught up in power games. If women are going to effect positive change, however, they can't stay away from the grimy political battlefields.

There will always be people who criticize no matter what a political figure does. Just be yourself—be sure to explain your positive motivations for running—and don't let pessimists and nay-sayers dim your own hopes and aspirations.

15

Evaluate statewide and congressional races differently from county and legislative contests. Such campaigns differ in intensity, visibility, complexity of issues, active constituencies, and nearly every way possible. It's the difference between standing on a hill facing a soft breeze versus jumping into the middle of a cyclone.

Expect a dramatic change of pace if you seek a state or congressional office. Even candidates with extensive experience in local and legislative campaigns are astounded by the demands of a state or congressional race.

Differences may include the number of hours a week required over a longer period of time (two or three years is not unusual); a monstrous campaign budget to be raised; out-of-town travel; an increased level of expectations regarding your long-term political plans and ambitions; the need for early polling and paid political consultant services; lack of a cohesive geographical unit for paid and free media coverage; larger campaign staffs who operate at further distance from the candidate; the need for a higher degree of polish and connections. You could manage a mom and pop grocery store, but what about Safeway International?

The most viable candidates for higher office are usually current local elected officials with name familiarity and proven track records.* Seeking a state or congressional office may require you to give up your comfortable position, a difficult choice if losing would leave you unemployed.

Congresswoman Louise Slaughter of New York initially declined to seek an open congressional seat in 1984 because she had unseated an incumbent county legislator only after three tries and was "painfully aware" of what she would give up if she entered the congressional race and lost. Two years later, displeased with the record of the person who won, she waged a winning campaign to oust him, the only woman in the country to beat an incumbent in 1986. An analysis of who did and didn't run in those races, and why, is contained in the book *Political Ambition, Who Decides to Run for Congress*, by Linda L. Fowler and Robert McClure.

Potential candidates need money in the bank to be considered viable, even before they announce their candidacy. A rule of thumb is that 10% of your total budget needs to be raised before a major donor will take you seriously. Most candidates for congressional and gubernatorial office test their ability to attract national money by journeying to the nation's capital to visit PACs and partisan campaign committees, although, in the end, the best sources of money for most challengers are closer to home.

It's important to test the incumbent's popularity and the mesh of his or her issues with voter attitudes before jumping into a major race. Even if your signs are favorable, don't expect to organize a large campaign the same way you did a campaign for a lower-level office. It's a different ball game.

---

* It is interesting to note, however, that neither Nita Lowey of New York in 1988 nor Joan Kelly Horn of Missouri in 1990 had previously held elective office. They were the sole women in those election years to unseat an incumbent member of Congress. Both ran against opponents with dubious records.

16

"For the last quarter century, American politics has been dominated by divisive, manipulative and largely phony debates about cultural and social issues—and the American people are weary," says E.J. Dionne Jr., author of *Why Americans Hate Politics*. He says the public still believes that the purpose of politics is "to solve problems and resolve disputes, but that is exactly what politics is not doing."

Voters credit female candidates with higher moral and ethical standards than male politicians; that's a start. If you have experience working with advocacy groups or serving on citizens' advisory boards and commissions, it will help prepare you for the voter-education role a candidate should automatically assume. More people need to be brought into the political process, laws governing ethical conduct of office holders need to be strengthened, voter apathy and anger must be acknowledged and overcome. "Take Back The System," is the rallying cry of the League of Women Voters of the United States.

You should also consider educating middle-class individuals, especially women, about the need to contribute money to political campaigns, no matter how modest the amount. Some groups to whom you speak may not want to hear this message; they may interpret it as too personal and partisan. If you talk about it under the general umbrella of the need for campaign reform, however, most people will be willing to listen.

Before Geraldine Ferraro ran for office, she presented a woman candidate with a $50 check, thinking she was being generous. Ferraro later realized her naivete when her husband wrote out a $1,000 check for a male candidate without batting an eye.

Gloria Steinem asks women, "Does your checkbook support your values?" Focus on that idea when you talk to women. Ask them: How much did you pay for the shoes you're wearing, your purse, your sweater? Are you contributing a reasonable portion of your hard-earned money, say 10%, toward causes which support your values? Is a quarter of that going toward electing officials who support women's issues or earmarked for electing good women candidates at the local, state, and congressional levels?

17

Expect the unexpected; happenstance is part of the game of politics. Be flexible and prepared to roll with the punches. Know that unexpected opponents can appear anytime, up to and including filing deadline day; vacancies occur unexpectedly and unrelated events can heavily influence the outcome of a race.

Anticipating who your opponents will be, both in the primary and general, is a gamble. Until filing day, the lineup is never certain. Even after filing day, dropouts can occur for critical health or personal reasons, even when a name remains on the ballot. Political and economic events totally out of your control can win or lose your race for you.

When Congresswoman Claudine Schneider gave up her safe House seat to challenge Rhode Island's senior senator, Claiborne Pell, no one foresaw that U.S. troops would be amassed near the Iraqi border in the Persian Gulf by the fall of 1990. Widely considered the woman most likely to beat an incumbent U.S. Senator, Schneider lost, at least partly because Pell was the ranking member of the Senate Foreign Policy Committee.

In Kansas, State Treasurer Joan Finney won two surprise gubernatorial victories in 1990—first the primary, then the general. She was outspent more than 3 to 1 by a former two-term Republican governor, but a strong property-tax revolt combined with anti-incumbency feelings helped propel her into office.

A wave of unprecedented opportunity for political newcomers may occur if new term-limitation measures are upheld by the courts. There are nearly half a million elected officials in the United States.* States across the country are considering measures similar to ones passed in Oklahoma, California, and Colorado in 1990.

---

* Exactly how many local elected officials serve is unknown. There are 535 members of Congress; 330 statewide elected officials; 7,461 state legislators; 102,329 governing boards of municipalities; possibly as many as 350,000 members of local school boards and special fire, water, sewer, lighting, street, sidewalk, park and other local improvement districts. (This does *not* include Democratic and Republican elected precinct committee persons, who are not government officials.) In *Winning Local and State Elections*, Ann Beaudry and Bob Schaeffer estimate that over 450,000 offices are up for election every two years.

Elections or appointments to fill vacancies (resignation or death of the incumbent) call for quick action. Be careful not to close off your options too quickly when a vacancy occurs, as Virginia Delegate Karen Darner discovered in late 1990.

When Delegate Warren Stambaugh died suddenly before Thanksgiving, Darner learned the day after the funeral that his widow intended to seek his office. Friends urged Darner to get in the race, but she thought, "I really can't oppose her at a time like this," even though Darner was much better known and had lived in the district much longer than Rosemary, who was Stambaugh's second wife. Rosemary Stambaugh's credentials were good, but Darner's were outstanding: past president of the Arlington League of Women Voters and of the Mental Health Association of Northern Virginia, a past state senate aide, a tireless campaign worker, recipient of awards for civic involvement, and more.

Because Darner initially said "no" and waited a few days before getting into the race, she lost the endorsement of most elected officials, who had already agreed to support Stambaugh before Darner made the decision to run. In spite of this, Darner won the Democratic Caucus nomination and went on to win the special election against an anti-choice Republican nominee. In Darner's case, losing the pre-caucus endorsements was not as critical as it would have been in an appointive process or in a regular election.

Judges often seek reelection and then resign in mid-term so their successors can be appointed rather than elected. The appointee is then entitled to use the word "incumbent" beside his or her name on the next ballot in states which allow such designations, a major advantage. To win a judicial appointment, women candidates need to lobby and line up support in much the same way endorsements are sought for a regular election, except that the focus for an appointment must be the appropriate appointing authority, usually the governor.

18

> *Recognize that deciding when and if to run is the hardest, and most important, decision you will make.* Timing is everything, both for making up your mind and for letting others know of your plans. Keep your vacillations out of the press unless you are deliberately hoisting a trial balloon. Your future efforts may not be taken seriously if you're viewed as a perennial candidate.

Give yourself a deadline for making up your mind. Don't ponder forever. The questions you need to resolve are three:

- Do you have what it takes to be a candidate—the stamina, the vision, the drive?
- Is your race winnable?
- Can you raise the money?

If your answers are "yes," or nearly so, it's time to take the leap of faith and run. How will you know whether or not you can do it if you don't try? The First Law in *The Seven Laws of Money* is, "Do it! Money will come when you are doing the right thing." Author Michael Phillips says this is the hardest law for people to accept.

Other words to contemplate:

A woman should share in the passion and action of her time at peril of being judged not to have lived.   --Oliver Wendell Holmes, Jr., 1884
(Pronoun and its antecedent modified)

Four things come not back: the spoken word, the sped arrow, time past, the neglected opportunity.   --Omar ibn al-Halif

Before actually filing (as opposed to *announcing* your candidacy), consider whether or not to file by petition. Some jurisdictions require signed petitions; others allow petitions as an alternative to paying a filing fee. Check with your local elections official to find out what the basic requirements and options are in your area.

Collecting names on a petition puts you on doorsteps and street corners, a marvelous way to win voter support from Day One. Everyone who signs his or her name will have a vested interest in seeing you elected. A minimum number of signatures is usually required but there's no limit on the maximum. Petitions can be an excellent way to kick off your campaign.

TIPS 19 - 30
Money and Fund-Raising

19

Your first job: Get money.

Thirty to 60% of your time as a candidate will be spent raising funds, possibly more. A successful first-time candidate for county office recently devoted 85% of his time to fund raising. Find out how much contestants for positions similar to yours spent in the past two elections to arrive at a target figure.

The cost of local campaigns tripled during the years from 1974 to 1990, while congressional races soared 10 times. In 1974, the average Congressional race cost $52,000; by 1990, the amount had escalated to $500,000.

Most small local elections still cost less than $10,000; many less than half that amount. An uncontested race could cost virtually nothing, but candidates who want to run again in the future should consider having their name on the ballot as an opportunity to gain name familiarity and plan to mount a modest advertising campaign. The demands of a small campaign differ vastly from those of high-visibility, contested races, of course. If you run against an opponent with name familiarity at any level, you will need more money than otherwise.

Don't fall for the alluring notion that you can win a race on grass roots support alone. Utilizing volunteers costs money.

A relatively new source of financial support for women candidates comes from women's political action committees. The oldest and largest bipartisan PAC for progressive women candidates is the Women's Campaign Fund (WCF) operating out of Washington, D.C., founded in 1974.

A PAC formed in 1986 called EMILY's List ("Early Money Is Like Yeast, it makes the dough rise") contributed $1.4 million to pro-choice Democratic women candidates for congressional and gubernatorial seats in 1990. Members all across the country paid $100 to join, then contributed at least $200 each election cycle to individual candidates recommended by EMILY's List.

No Republican women's PAC equivalent to EMILY's List had been formed at the time of this writing, although a Women's Senate Republican Victory Committee (WSRVC), was formed as a joint fund-raising endeavor in 1990 by the six Republican women who ran for the U.S. Senate that year. The WSRVC was run in conjunction with the National Republican Senatorial Committee (NRSC) and may or may not be reestablished in the future.

The National Women's Political Caucus (NWPC), organized in the early '70s, continues to be a strong source of technical, moral, and financial support for women candidates. Political action committees of the National Organization for Women (NOW) and the National Abortion Rights Action League (NARAL) have become increasingly active in recent years in recruiting and supporting women candidates. All three of these PACs are bipartisan. The Fund for a Feminist Majority, an offshoot of NOW, is playing a major role in getting more young women involved in the political process and has targeted college campuses for its work.

By 1990, at least 35 women's PACs were operating across the United States, in addition to local PACs affiliated with national organizations like NWPC and NOW. About half of the 35 were in California, including two new PACs aimed specifically toward Hispanic issues and Hispanic women in politics.* The Hollywood Women's Political Committee (HWPC) received national publicity by raising $1.5 million at a $5,000 per couple dinner hosted by Barbra Streisand.

(Not all of the money raised by these PACs goes to female candidates; some goes to male candidates who support women's issues. The names and addresses of most women's PACs can be obtained from the Center for the American Woman in Politics (CAWP) at Rutgers University. Addresses and telephone numbers for all of the above organizations and four national pro-choice PACs are listed in the appendix.)

In addition to financial aid, women's PACs provide technical advice and moral support. Some do research and polling. Others provide an

---

* The first Hispanic elected to the Los Angeles County Board of Supervisors in over a hundred years was Gloria Molino, in early 1991. In 1982, Molino was the first Hispanic elected to the California legislature, with 75% of her contributions coming from women and women's groups, according to *Women as Candidates in American Politics*. The first Latina and Cuban-American woman was elected to Congress in mid-1990—Republican Congresswoman Ileana Ros-Lehtinen of Florida who replaced U.S. Rep. Claude Pepper after his death. The Hispanic Caucus Chair of the National Women's Political Caucus, Anita Perez Ferguson of California, planned a rerun in 1992 for the Congressional seat she lost to the incumbent by only a 6% edge in 1990.

opportunity for women candidates to get to know each other, to gather as a group and share experiences, both during and after their campaigns.

Correlated phenomena are the fund-raising efforts by individual elected women officials who in turn make contributions to other campaigns. Oregon's powerful Speaker of the House, Vera Katz, raised over $190,000 during the 1989-90 cycle with no opponent, and approximately $125,000 the previous election cycle with only token opposition. She contributed most of this money to other Democratic candidates, including aspiring women. (Legislators in some states are working to prohibit transfer of funds from one candidate to another in the future.)

20

Face the fact that you must be a salesperson to raise needed funds for a campaign. The product you sell is yourself. If you can't face the prospect of repeating a sales pitch innumerable times, don't enter a major race. Remember to thank your contributors; it paves the way for the next sale.

Picking up the telephone and making the first call is the hardest part; but like skating, once you get rolling, it's not that hard.

Your personal fund-raising efforts will focus principally on one-on-one telephone calls and appointments, and appearances before groups which endorse and give money to candidates. Volunteers and staff members can make calls for events, but the continuous, ongoing, never-ending phone calls for big dollars must be built into your routine like eating and sleeping. No one else can raise money as effectively as the candidate.

Set aside a block of at least two or three hours every day to make fund-raising calls. You will be calling from lists prepared by staff or volunteers. Research about prior contributors to races like yours is an important campaign component. You need to know how much money to ask for and which candidates the person you call has supported in the past.

For best results, have your campaign manager or a finance committee member sit in the room with you while you make those calls. This is a common practice for both male and female candidates.

Have a basic script in front of you: Explain why you're running and why you have a good chance of winning; ask for a large and specific amount. Professional fund-raisers say people are never insulted by being asked for too much money. Then wait for an answer, don't rush in and let the potential donor off the hook.

Don't be apologetic when you ask for money, a common tendency for women candidates. Market yourself positively: You are the best candidate. You will be an excellent public official. You are confident, you are strong, you are a good leader. You have the power to win and to excel. Contributing money is a way in which other people can take part in that process.

For a successful fund-raising session you need to know your lines, to be "up" for it—to feel an energy, a commitment, a winning charge which will convey itself across the telephone lines. It's like preparing for battle—one needs to be psychologically alert, ready for combat, ready to fend off possible attacks, convinced you're going to win.

It's very important that you ask for a specific amount. Have the person sitting in with you write down commitments made, note address changes and follow up with a thank-you letter and pledge envelope. For large pledges, ask the donor if it would be convenient for someone to pick up the check and when.

Making "cold calls" to people you've never met is the hardest. Using someone else's name as an entry wedge will give you a sense of standing and credibility.

Volunteer Bob Weil, a good-natured retired executive, assisted Oregon Governor Barbara Roberts for six months in 1990 while she made her fund-raising calls which raised $2 million. Her "appointments" were scheduled from 10 to 15 minutes apart, people were expecting her calls so it was vital to keep on schedule—a difficult thing for a "people person" like Roberts who loves to talk.

Campaign Manager Patricia McCaig told Weil, "Get her off the phone and onto the next call—make her stop talking!" One of the techniques Weil used was to make up black and white race track signal flags and wave them in front of Roberts the next time her conversation went on too long—and of course sending Roberts into gales of laughter.

Whole books are written on the subject of fund raising. Week-long courses are devoted to the topic. You can find experienced volunteers to give you advice and/or hire a professional fund-raising consultant. See sources for further study in the appendix.

21

Decide the limits of your family financial support, whether or not you can tolerate unpaid debts, and how expenditure commitments will be monitored. Emotions run so high in the heat of a campaign that family decisions about maximum financial outlay must be made before you get into the race. Either rule out family support or deliberately set aside a dollar amount for investment and possible loss. Designate some person outside the campaign staff, such as the treasurer, to approve and monitor expenditures and track outstanding unpaid bills and items ordered but not yet received.

Some candidates shun the idea of making loans to the campaign or of going into personal debt. However, donors may see the presence or lack of personal funds in the race as a sign of your own convictions. The only reason women shouldn't spend their own money if they wish to and can afford to is the possible negative image of trying to "buy" an election. However, that is not nearly as big a danger as an empty campaign account with unpaid bills. Many vendors, having been burned in the past, won't give credit to political campaigns and demand cash on the line before delivery.

Gubernatorial candidates Dianne Feinstein of California and Arliss Sturgulewski of Alaska both made major contributions or loans to their campaigns. Feinstein and her husband put in $3 million in the early days of her 1990 race. U.S. Senator Nancy Kassebaum launched her first primary race on $90,000 of her own money in 1978. Jack Kennedy's father not only contributed thousands of dollars to his son's first campaign for Congress, but spent countless hours convincing his friends and acquaintances to do likewise.

Even for winning candidates, paying off debts is no fun. It's much harder raising money for a deficit than for the race itself; many candidates end up paying off such amounts personally over a number of years. However, there are times in nearly every campaign when printing bills are due and media deposits have to be made or something will get cancelled. Most medium-to-large campaigns have to borrow at least once during the campaign, usually for cash-in-advance media space. If you may need to borrow, make inquiries long before the money must be in hand.

22

Scrutinize the budget your campaign manager proposes; the primary burden of raising the money to meet its goals will be yours. Don't be reluctant to be seen as a penny-pinching female when paring the budget. Plan alternative budgets A, B, and C tied to incremental fund-raising goals. Identify dates when spending will be curtailed if agreed-upon scenarios aren't realized.

The budget is an integral part of the overall campaign plan and should include projections of income and expense, by month, for the entire campaign. Generally, 60% to 80% of your money should be reserved for advertising and voter contact materials. The main variable in A, B, and C budgets will be your advertising dollars; it is difficult to reduce fixed commitments.

A common campaign mistake is to allow early fixed costs such as salaries and benefits, rent, phones, and computers to eat up so much money there is not enough left for advertising. A rule of thumb is to keep fixed costs to 20% of your budget total, even for small campaigns.*

Contributors don't like to think that they're paying for staff salaries, perhaps a hold-over from the days when women didn't have paid jobs and campaigns could count on almost full-time volunteers. Staff salaries are also invisible and indirect; people can't see their effect and don't like to pay for something they can't see.

You must get your name before the voters—whether by direct mail, billboards, radio, newspaper ads, television, or by other innovative methods like renting an organ grinder or hot air balloon. Printing and postage costs can be monumental; this is frequently an under-budgeted item. Ask a recent candidate what his or her printing and postage costs actually were so you can be prepared.

Every organized campaign needs a coordinator or manager, preferably with a salary attached, possibly half-time for a small race. The amount of salary should be decided before anyone is hired, and once set, is very

---

* However, if you have more committed volunteers available to you than money, you may decide to budget more than 20% for fixed costs, mainly in staff, so you can conduct a grassroots person-to-person campaign to exploit your strengths. Major grassroots organizing is more staff intensive than a media campaign.

difficult to reduce. A few candidates offer a basic salary plus a bonus if he or she wins. However, the American Association of Political Consultants frowns on this practice as unethical: your contributors and advisors may, too. It could also cause you to exceed campaign spending limitations.

Find a reliable person to look after campaign finances—someone flexible, but firm. Accurate records must be kept. In states which require the reporting of aggregate contributions by groups or individuals, the use of a computer can be a life-saver. If you cannot find a volunteer treasurer whom you personally know to be reliable, hire a professional to manage your accounts and do your official reporting. You as the candidate are ultimately responsible for raising the money being spent, for reporting it accurately, and for unpaid campaign debts. You could be fined for mistakes made in your name.

Ask your treasurer to prepare a biweekly or monthly comparison of actual to budgeted income and expense by categories so you can know exactly how your campaign is faring. Even if the campaign office does not have a computer, your financial records could be kept separately by the treasurer or another responsible individual who has computer access. That person could generate financial information for campaign use as well as official reports required by law, using common spreadsheet software, assuming your state allows such formats. Special requirements may apply for reporting of PAC contributions.

23

Find a financial angel. Probe your memory and search creatively for someone who might champion your candidacy financially. The mentor every candidate dreams of is a committed supporter with no business-related interest in your race who has close ties to generous financial contributors. Few female candidates have such contacts and will need to cultivate them.

Some candidates have financial backers they met through cultural events or arts associations—boards for symphony, opera, art museum, and ballet organizations. Family ties can be most productive of all. Other valuable connections come through organizations like University Clubs, Business Clubs, City Clubs, Kiwanis—any group which draws influential and affluent members. With women pushing open the doors of formerly all-male bastions across the country (citing local property-tax exemptions and IRS regulations which allow such groups favorable treatment), more opportunities are becoming available to women to tap into "old boy networks," the traditional sources of campaign funds.

Be careful not to appear too dependent on any one source of dollars. If it looks improper it could become a campaign issue for your opponent—appearance is often as important as reality in politics. If you become known as the mouthpiece or supporter of one person or cause, you will lose credibility and objectivity for dealing with the countless other issues which will come before you.

What do donors expect in return for large contributions? Usually they want recognition: being thanked, getting a complementary ticket to an event, getting appointed to a Blue Ribbon committee, perhaps sitting at a head table or being included in a special reception. Contributors expect you to be a competent public official who does her homework, who is fair, and who has an open mind. Major donors may expect you to take their phone calls occasionally and listen to their complaints and suggestions, but only clods presume to buy your vote or control your actions.

If you think there may be unacceptable strings attached to any gift, return the money before it goes into your bank account. The Sixth Law in *The Seven Laws of Money* says: "You can never really receive money as a gift....A gift of money is really a contract...and it requires performance and an accounting of performance that is satisfactory to the giver." Be sure you understand if there are any expectations by major contributors beyond your performance of the duties of your office to the best of your abilities.

"It is the nature of man," Florentine wrote five centuries ago, "to feel as much bound by the favors they do as by those they receive." A *New York Times* book review of the novel *Victories* notes that "while people are eternally forgetful of favors done for them, they rarely forget the favors they have done for others." In *Victories*, a neophyte politician learns the value of seeking and accepting favors from others, which gives them a vested stake in his career.

24

Get "in-kind" contributions to keep cash outlay down. Securing free headquarters space should be a high priority. Federal campaign laws and most state laws require the reporting of in-lieu-of-cash contributions such as photocopying, printing, graphics, retail value of rental space, food for events outside of the home, wine and beer (if local laws allow), vehicle or airplane use, loaned executives, etc. Some people will contribute goods or space or services, but not cash. Most campaigns waste needed dollars on non-voter-contact items which could be donated.

Many individuals and businesses who would never consider writing out a check will willingly make an in-kind contribution, either by donating merchandise, free labor, or providing something at discounted cost. Any time you pay less than the usual and normal charge, you receive something of value which is reportable as a campaign contribution under Federal campaign laws and most state election laws.* Many of your supporters undoubtedly have items sitting in their garages, basements, and family rooms which could be used by the campaign.

When scouting for donated campaign headquarters, look for vacant storefronts or office space, free parking, accessible public transportation in an area safe for volunteers to come and go by day and night. Find out where previous candidates have had their headquarters. Call around to realtors. Your campaign will look and feel more professional if it is located somewhere other than a personal residence. Be sure the space contains adequate electrical outlets for computers and typewriters, and, if possible, existing wiring for a reasonably-priced telephone system. The in-kind value of donated headquarters can be substantial—$10,000 to $20,000 a year is not uncommon.

In addition to the examples cited above, an auction of donated items and services can be an outstanding fund-raising event with very low overhead. Restaurants contribute certificates for lunch or dinner, friends offer sailboat rides, local artists contribute paintings, elected officials

---

* Many corporate in-kind and other forms of contributions are prohibited by federal law and some state laws. Consult your local elections official and see the address for the Federal Elections Commission in the appendix.

agree to breakfast or golfing with the highest bidder. Auctions require massive work and coordination, but the pay-off can be fruitful. Portland Commissioner Gretchen Kafoury cleared $22,000 at such an auction in 1990.

Your campaign manager and driver-aide should carry with them a list of office supplies and other campaign necessities—writing pads—waste baskets—audio tapes—VCR tapes—cookies—file folders—and solicit in-kind contributions. Post the list prominently at campaign headquarters where everyone can see it.

25

Ask everyone for money; no one gives unless they're asked. Search your files and recollections for names of people you and your family know who may be potential contributors. Tracking down addresses and phone numbers is not easy, so start early, early, early. Individuals and groups are out there, willing and able to send you money, provided you ask.

Campaigns which don't raise enough money haven't asked enough people, enough times, in enough different ways.

Most people are never asked for money. Many people will give if asked personally by a candidate they know.

Start maintaining lists of possible volunteers and contributors as soon as you think you might someday run. For a full-time paid City Council race, compile a list of 50 people who could each give you $100. For congressional races make the figure $1,000; for a county commissioner race, say $50. For a volunteer position in a small town, make it $10. If available, analyze lists of contributors to other candidates to find out what the level of giving averages in your kind of race. Also ask your relatives, especially your spouse, to prepare lists of potential donors.

When Clackamas County (Oregon) Commissioner Darlene Hooley first ran for the state legislature, she wrote down the names of *everyone* she knew, including the Avon Lady and a neighbor she didn't think liked her. At the mailing party when volunteers were addressing her first fund-raising letter, Hooley said, "Oh, don't bother to send to them, it's not worth the stamps." But somehow the letters got mailed. To her surprise, Hooley received $100 from each of them. Other people Hooley assumed would send her money never did. Don't exclude anyone from your list unless they're supporting your opponent.

Always include a return envelope with written solicitation letters and, for best results, have a caller follow up the request. Don't be shy about asking people more than once; it sometimes takes repeated requests before people respond.

The candidate's personal telephone calls will usually be limited to those seeking more than $50, $100, or $200, depending upon the size of the campaign budget. Calls for lesser amounts will be delegated to others. Don't worry about asking too high. No one is hurt because you think they are successful.

End all telephone solicitations on a positive note if possible, no matter what you've asked for or how unfriendly the "no." Some people unaccustomed to giving are embarrassed to be asked, and don't know how to give a graceful refusal. Don't take it personally if someone says no—maybe their child is in therapy or they have some other private financial pressure you don't know about. They may also later change their minds if they have been treated with courtesy and haven't been alienated by the call.

Writing solicitation letters is almost a science, as you can tell from examples which arrive in your own mail box. Start saving these letters and analyze them. Which ones do you personally find most appealing? Obtain samples of other candidates' fund-raising letters. Seek professional assistance (paid or volunteer) in drafting an effective appeal.

Expect grumbling from friends and supporters about the duplicate solicitations they get from your campaign. You simply can't avoid it. You may wish to add a note at the bottom of your mass solicitations letters saying, "If you receive more than one copy of this letter, please pass it on to a friend." And don't overlook asking your volunteers to contribute. Even if the amount is small, consider making it a campaign goal to put every volunteer's name on your donor list.

Candidates for judgeships have to be more careful in their efforts to secure funding than do other candidates, because they are prohibited from personally soliciting money by Canons of Ethics. However, nothing prohibits committees from soliciting money on a judicial candidate's behalf.

Advice for women candidates in general applies to women seeking judgeships. In addition, Codes of Judicial Conduct generally specify that judicial candidates must refrain from political activity inappropriate to the judicial office, avoid taking positions on ballot measures or other disputed public issues, not attend partisan fund-raising events, refrain from mentioning a partisan political affiliation. Judicial candidates may usually appear at candidate fairs to be introduced, but some states prohibit their appearance at fund-raising events for partisan candidates. Check with your local bar association or state supreme court for specifics.

26 *Be prepared for a fund-raising event at which nobody shows. It's part of the territory; don't let it get you down. Advance ticket sales can help assure covering basic expenses, but won't be the same morale booster as a well-attended party. Have a policy about whether or not to issue complementary tickets, and to whom, to assure a minimum crowd. Keep expenses low to avoid big losses.*

It happens to everyone: the dreaded event for which nobody shows. Even powerful incumbents can be humiliated by a no-show event if the place or time is wrong or someone hasn't done enough advance work. Check dates with other organizations to avoid conflicts.

The details of fund-raising events must be carefully monitored. "What can go wrong, will go wrong." Campaign manuals contain examples of planning worksheets for events that should be followed religiously. See appendix.

Choose locations for your events that are smaller than you think you'll need, rather than vice versa. Your crowd will look larger, and people like being a bit squashed together at a party. Adjoining space for spill-over or quiet conversations is ideal.

Phenomenal fund-raising events resemble religious revival meetings. Testimonials and entertainment are followed by emotional pleas for money. Shills planted at strategic spots in the audience proclaim pledges of $200, $500 and $1,000, with attendants passing through the audience to pick up checks and pledge cards. It's pure salesmanship and theater, and very, very effective.

Make sure that all guests are greeted warmly at campaign events, and assign someone to make sure that major donors are not left standing or sitting off by themselves, a not-infrequent occurrence. An initial contribution may be turned into an even larger one later or the donor may agree to serve as a loan guarantor at a crucial point in the campaign.

After greeting people individually, the candidate always says a few words to the assembled guests at every party, large or small. People like to see their candidate on center stage and a short speech gives the occasion a feeling of unity and purpose.

27

Project the image of a winner; people contribute to WINNING campaigns. Favorable poll results are the best way to convince potential donors that you are a winner. An upward trend in polls carries weight, as does evidence of a well-organized campaign and endorsements by key individuals, organizations, and newspapers.

On the phone, in the mail, in person, what potential contributors want to know is: What are your chances? They're saying, "Convince me that you're going to win and I'll send you money."

The winner image also comes across in a crowd. Have committed supporters in every audience; don't be shy about having two or three who will lead the group in a standing ovation if the opportunity presents itself. Such displays of enthusiasm help convince the media that your campaign is on a roll, which in turn inspires donors to open up their checkbooks.

Geraldine Ferraro became adept at giving audiences the emotional experience they sought at rallies. D.C. Mayor Sharon Pratt Dixon is another example of a firebrand behind the mike. Texas Governor Ann Richards, a witty, dynamic speaker, gave the keynote address at the 1988 Democratic National Convention while serving as State Treasurer and gained national attention in doing so.

Bandwagons for political candidates have been compared to parades, circuses, floods, religious revivals, rock concerts, trains on well-oiled tracks. Certainly an element beyond rational choice is involved at the ballot box. Ronald Reagan was called the "perfect candidate" for his ability to touch people's lives, to convince voters of his sincerity and to evoke a loyal following.

"Has (the Democratic party) forgotten that freewheeling, sometimes raucous, sometimes hyperbolic speech is the essence of political rhetoric?" syndicated columnist Jeff Greenfield asked when Democrats were reacting with "virtue outraged" to Reagan's successes. "And has it forgotten how to answer in kind?" Roosevelt and Truman relished political combat, Greenfield reminded his readers.

If making fiery speeches fits your personality, do it! If not, utilize other less theatrical ways of letting people know that your campaign is on the winning track.

28

Have cash on hand to pay for media buys well in advance. The FCC allows stations to demand payment for political TV and radio spots a week before airing; billboards and bench ads usually require deposits several weeks in advance with full payment before posting. Advertising agencies and local stations will pressure you for early money. Such payments come due before the visible part of campaigning occurs, a difficult time to secure contributions.

Federal laws require that television and radio stations treat all candidates equally, which for practical purposes means that all candidates pay for political advertising in advance, usually a week before airing of the first spot. Agencies must sign a contract to reserve time and often their relationship with the media is on the line, says political consultant Julie Williamson. The agency wants your money early enough to cancel, if you're not going to be able to come up with the dollars, so the media won't be left with unsold time they could have sold to others.

This requirement is tough for new candidates, a chicken and egg scenario in which seeing and hearing commercials motivates potential givers to actually send in their checks.

In the absence of paid consultant advice to the contrary, save your money for the last two, three, or four weeks before the election. Advertising money spent early is gone forever, and is no longer available for the crucial days when voters make up their minds. Harriett Woods' narrow loss in her 1986 Missouri race for U.S. Senate is often cited as an example of money spent too soon so that not enough was left near the end to refute and counterbalance her opponent's negative ads.

Missouri Congresswoman Joan Kelly Horn believes that saving her money until the last three weeks of her 1990 race won the race for her. She had a powerful message to deliver—an opponent with an unsavory track record which Horn exposed to the voters. (Doing so earlier would also have given him more time to counter-attack.)

Oregon Governor Barbara Roberts took the opposite tack. Her campaign put money into an early media blitz from mid-August to mid-September, a risky proposition. "That gutsy decision paid off," said Roberts in a *ProWOMAN* magazine interview. Roberts credited the early television campaign with "turning people around, turning the polls around, and giving the campaign the momentum it needed." Volunteers making fund-raising calls for her campaign attested to the excitement and motivation the ads generated. Her supporters needed proof she could win after political insiders and columnists had written her off.

Fund-raising efforts have to be planned so that money is in the bank when advertising has to be paid for. You may need to borrow money to meet deadlines for media buys. Pledges outstanding will help obtain loans, but your most likely source is a family member or a committed campaign supporter.

You can't wait till the week before TV and radio ads will run to decide whether or not to reserve the time. You must sign up two or three months in advance to get the best spots for your money. Your goal is to reserve the times best suited for your target audience.

29

Outspend your opponent; winning candidates almost always do. It is possible to beat an opponent with a much bigger budget than you, but the odds are against it. The top three predictors of a candidate's success are incumbency, amount of money spent, and name familiarity.

In spite of notable examples to the contrary, women's campaigns overall were better funded in 1990 than ever before. The playing field was more level, a sign that political insiders are recognizing the growing strength of female candidates. On the local level, women are often assumed to have arrived in politics; their candidacies are taken seriously and their fund-raising efforts are pulling even.

As recently as 1972, Elizabeth Holzman unseated incumbent New York Congressman Emanuel Celler in a Democratic district he had represented for fifty years. She was able to raise only $32,000 after being told she would need a minimum of $100,000 to run and that anyone could raise that much. (By 1990, the cost of the average House race had risen to $400,000.) Celler failed to take Holzman's challenge seriously. She attacked his poor attendance record, his support of the Vietnam War, his being out of touch with his district—and became the youngest woman ever elected to Congress. Holzman believes that the volunteer-based, shoe-leather campaign she waged would be exceedingly difficult, if not impossible, today, with congressional campaigns now dominated by television, a component only money can buy.

When Congresswoman Louise Slaughter successfully challenged a first-term incumbent in New York's 30th Congressional District in 1986, she raised $50,000 more than her opponent by the end of June of election year. This fund-raising capability made local headlines and convinced political insiders that she could win—thus releasing a tide of more money flowing in her direction.

One of the major reasons incumbents get reelected is because raising money is much easier for them than for challengers. While you don't always have to outspend your opponent, you have to raise enough to run a very visible race.

30 *Meet, during non-election years, with corporate executives who give money to other political candidates. Business men and women like to make the acquaintance of up-and-coming candidates when they aren't being asked for money. Ask three business leaders to host an off-year breakfast or luncheon for you, and later visit invitees who can't attend at their offices.*

The best time to make contact with businessmen and women in your community, civic movers and shakers, is in off-election years before your campaign begins.

The same businessman who will decline to see an unknown candidate during a campaign may welcome a visit in an off-year. Making such a call demonstrates your commitment and your potential, both attributes which are attractive to traditional political donors.

Female candidates need to work harder to develop relationships with business leaders than do male candidates because men dominate the business world and the informal networks inside that sphere. Contacts made in non-political environments are important ones. Identify key individuals and get to know them.

Quietly soliciting contributions during an off-election year is also an effective way to keep potential opponents out of your race. Nothing is more discouraging to others than a well-organized candidate with a huge war chest. And even though state laws differ on exact legal requirements, you are advised not to collect money until you have a special bank account to put it in and a political treasurer designated to safeguard its disposition.

TIPS 31 - 35

Campaign Structure and Campaign Manager

31

"There is no more important relationship than the one between the candidate and the campaign manager," says Rhode Island Secretary of State Kathleen Connell. "There has to be absolute trust and confidence. They should have a level of trust that allows them to fight hard without coming unstuck."

Connell's campaign manager Patricia Soares says: "You have to know the candidate well enough so that you can decide what is right for her to do in the campaign. A campaign manager's agenda must only be that of the candidate. Accessibility to the candidate is important, too. A campaign manager can't operate in a vacuum. She/he has to have at least one hour a week to meet with the candidate to discuss the campaign. The campaign manager must believe in the candidate and in her political agenda."

In smaller contests such as a low-key school board race, you might be your own campaign manager with a volunteer sidekick to hold the title and assist with details. (Some people say it is NEVER a good idea for a candidate to manage her own campaign, but quite a few candidates would never run if they had to wait for someone else willing and able to perform the campaign manager role, especially for little or no salary.) Consulting regularly with a close advisor who has extensive campaign experience is imperative for both a novice candidate and a novice campaign manager.

"The ideal manager is a twenty-four-hour-a-day support system, able to provide both emotional support and hard-nosed advice to a candidate who may need a kind word or, conversely, a tough critique," says Ruth Mandel in *In the Running: The New Woman Candidate*.

Finding such a person is not easy. Few experienced managers are available, and nothing teaches the hard lessons of political campaigns like experience. Recruiting staff for legislative and congressional candidates is often easier than for other campaigns because of the potential for full-time employment as an aide after the candidate assumes office.

Ignore gender as a criterion for a campaign manager; just find the best person available. While some people have the notion that female candidates need a male manager, others assume women candidates ought to practice what they preach and hire a woman for their top management role. Disregard both concepts: look for qualifications, check out references thoroughly, and find a good personality fit.

Management experience in the business world may come closest to providing needed campaign skills, but not everyone is suited to the hectic pace, stress, and shuffling deck of cards encountered in a political campaign. Campaign training schools are available if you hire someone by early fall of the year preceding an election. One-day campaign schools may also be available at the start of an election year.

Experienced campaign managers do not come cheap. On the national scene, the salary range was from $2,500 to $6,000 per month in 1990, sometimes with an apartment thrown into the bargain. The going rate for local managers varied from $1,000 to $5,000 per month in Oregon, depending on the size of the race. Note that these rates are for *experienced* campaign managers. You should not expect to pay a novice as much as you would offer a pro.

Your campaign manager should not be a surrogate candidate. He or she must be willing to stay in the office and work, not spend all his or her time hanging out with the candidate or shoring up contacts for other employment or laying the groundwork for a personal campaign sometime in the future.

Hiring old friends or family members, no matter how loyal or well intentioned, isn't the answer. Most people would be out of their depth and such relationships are difficult to keep on a business-like basis. However, family members have performed those duties with distinction in the past: witness former Congresswoman Lindy Boggs, who managed her husband's campaigns before his death and before she herself ran; Mario Cuomo's son, Andrew; Jack Kennedy's brother, Bobby.

The general rule, however, is to keep family and loyal friends out of the management and strategy side of the campaign and to utilize their services in other ways. A close friend could be an ideal volunteer coordinator for a small campaign; she already knows your friends and could gently twist their arms on your behalf.

32

Set parameters for how much or how little you will personally be involved in the details of the campaign. **Your degree of involvement will depend on the size and pace of the race plus your personality and that of your campaign manager. Some candidates insist on writing their own speeches, others want only a weekly briefing about what's going on at headquarters.**

An essential ingredient in a good working relationship is that the candidate and her manager be absolutely clear about their expectations of one another. No candidate has time to clutter her mind with details, yet women candidates are vulnerable to the charge that they don't delegate enough, that they are unwilling to let loose of things. Without realizing it, staff members don't always extend the same automatic authority to women candidates as they do to men; they don't trust female political instincts and judgments, and are more apt to object to an authoritarian style coming from a woman.

A good way to clarify expectations is to specify the campaign manager's range of authority in writing. Designate which processes require the candidate's approval before being finalized: Press releases? Fund-raising letters? Questionnaires? Brochures? Photos? Stipulate that everything not listed falls in the campaign manager's domain.

Just because they're written down doesn't mean job duties are chiseled in stone. Responsibilities may well shift with the flow of the campaign. It is also possible that the candidate in a small-to-medium-sized campaign may have to step in and take control of the campaign if her manager is floundering. The train won't wait; it will pull out of the station and your campaign crew had better be on it no matter who has to herd the stragglers on board.

When there is full-time paid staff, things a candidate should not be involved in include choosing graphic designs and layouts, getting out mailings, addressing envelopes, ordering and picking up print orders and office supplies, writing letters (except notes at the bottom of form letters), receiving or opening campaign mail.

Former San Francisco Mayor Dianne Feinstein believes candidates need to keep the upper hand in campaigns, that not to do so is a major sign of weakness. "Hell hath no fury like a man fired by a woman," Feinstein said when her long-time political consultant quit (August 1989, during her 1990 California gubernatorial race) and faxed a press release to the media accusing her of not being willing to make commitments about the campaign.

The thin line between abdication of responsibility and letting go so others can do their jobs has to be walked very carefully. "You can judge a candidate by her campaign," is a commonly-accepted statement. People will judge your potential performance in office by how smoothly and effectively your campaign runs. If the campaign fouls up, you get the public blame, not your manager or consultant or other staff. The campaign is being run using your good name. You have to be sure that that good name is guarded well.

While you must delegate, you must also monitor the campaign's progress. Your job as a candidate is to raise money, meet voters, and know your issues. The campaign manager's job is to take care of everything else. If things aren't being done to your satisfaction, let your campaign manager know, possibly through a third party (see next tip.) Your manager must also tell *you* when you are not doing your job (again, possibly through a third party), and you must be ready to listen.

33

Decide what purpose and role your steering committee will play before you ask people to serve. Keep authority for campaign policy decisions within a tight circle of three to five people. Some advisory committees are simply "flash" names to lend credibility to the candidate, others are made up of individuals with campaign responsibilities who seldom meet and who don't make decisions.

A broad-based advisory group with honorary status for "name-only" members to give credibility to the campaign, along with an executive committee to make decisions, can work well. Candidates in smaller races sometimes operate solely with ad hoc committees and advisors, using their "flash" names for quotes in campaign literature.

You should have a "kitchen cabinet," or small decision-making circle of three to five people to include at least yourself, your campaign manager, and an objective, knowledgeable third party whom you trust. You and your campaign manager may both be opinionated, hard drivers who need a cool-headed tie-breaker to keep your relationship steady. (Exclude your spouse unless your manager has agreed to his inclusion before signing on. However, in a race without a paid manager or consultant, a spouse may be a key advisor or even run the campaign.)

People who comprise your kitchen cabinet should have complementary strengths, including familiarity with the campaign organization and the race, knowledge of the district, understanding of your personal strengths and weaknesses, management and personnel experience, proven political savvy, distance from daily campaign activity, and basic common sense.

Whatever you do, don't let a group of inexperienced people vote on strategy. Campaign management is not a democracy! And don't become dependent on half a dozen telephone advisors who each have strong opinions which they want to pass on to you personally and who never meet face to face. Choose one main advisor, a paid consultant or one of your kitchen cabinet members, to be your strategy czar. Have that person be the focal point for calls from people who have advice for the campaign.

An example of the kind of question a steering committee might give feedback on is how to present your name in the campaign logo and literature. How will the name look, and sound? Women candidates are often advised to emphasize their first names for the warm personal, neighborly image that provides. A steering committee is also a good sounding board for testing reactions to brochures, controversial ads and issues under consideration.

A committee member with personnel and management experience may be able to mediate differences between you and your manager or between staff members, saving you stress and strain. A trusted steering committee member may be in a better position than the campaign manager to cajole a headstrong candidate into doing what she has to do.

Also beware the committee member, consultant, or staff member with a need to "own" or "run" the candidate. Some people have a need to wield power. A first-time candidate, a "greenhorn," is especially vulnerable to takeover.

Know yourself, your strengths, your short-comings. Compensate for your lacks through the people you choose to run your campaign and to be your close advisors.

34

Consider hiring a political consultant with broad campaign authority. Campaigns get more complex every year, partly because of increasing campaign budgets which draw talented resources to plot and chart and plan. Political consulting is a growing profession. Amateurs have difficulty competing with that kind of know-how.

"The book is still being written on how women should campaign," notes *Momentum: Women in American Politics NOW*, by Ronna Romney and Beppie Harrison. "Male chauvinism is not dead in the ranks of consultants, who are apt to see themselves as vastly more knowledgeable than any woman, even if she happens to be the candidate."

Which services to be performed by staff and which by consultants will depend on what part of the country you are from, the race you are in, and possibly what political party. Some Republican and Democratic committees and nonpartisan PACs provide professional services without cost to candidates in targeted races.

A consultant's reputation adds or detracts from campaign credibility, so experienced consultants have considerable bargaining power. A single political consultant located in the same geographical area occasionally acts as campaign manager for two or three small campaigns at once, with on-site managers overseeing office activities under the consultant's tutelage. The consultant/manager handles strategy, writes the campaign plan, arranges for polling and consults on polling questions, arranges for the design of mailing pieces and printing, and writes or contracts for radio and TV spots. In other circumstances, those specialties would be handled by separate consultants and the campaign manager would coordinate their services.

The biggest controversy regarding political consultants usually occurs between out-of-state firms and their clients. Candidates question whether consultants who direct activities by telephone from hundreds of miles away really understand their districts. Particularly troublesome are the winner's bonuses some of these firms insist upon.

One legislative candidate who signed a contract in 1990 providing for a winner's bonus to a consulting firm says she would never do it again. Her agreement specified a payment of $10,000 if she won, and her opponent in the small-town rural district made a big issue of it. Voters didn't like the bonus idea—it sounded unethical, as if some kind of bribery were involved. The assumption that a winner could easily obtain lobbyist contributions also left a tainted image in the voters' minds.

In deciding strategy for a legislative or lower-visibility race, your own "gut" feelings may be more valid than those of an out-of-town consultant. You've been involved in the community, you know the constituency better than they. What plays in New York may not sit well in Iowa.

Also, "carpetbagger" consultant firms sometimes market their services broadly and take on more clients than they can stay with, then leave the candidate in the lurch a couple of months before election day if the campaign looks weak or the candidate hasn't raised big bucks for media buys. They don't stick around to dig in for a win. These consultants have no stake in the candidate or her community and are concerned mainly for their own win-loss record.

It comes back to the axiom, "All politics is local." Sometimes foreigners can misjudge the territory and you are better off relying on expertise closer to home. On the other hand, if there is no experienced political strategist nearby who has time available and who fits your political bent and personality, you may have no choice but to go with an out-of-state firm. If you start inquiring early, you will find that various options are available and not feel forced into an unsuitable relationship.

35 *Expect some staff and volunteer turnover early in the campaign.* **Every new organization goes through a shakedown period. Turnover is especially prevalent in first-time campaigns; some workers don't fit the needs of the job, others have romantic expectations far different from the reality.**

Job qualifications should be the primary criteria for choosing staff, but loyalty to the candidate plays a role. Qualities to look for in staff include a sense of humor, good organization skills and follow-through, friendly demeanor, common sense, commitment to the candidate and her campaign, willingness and ability to work overtime.

It takes a while for campaign workers to settle in, for the candidate and her staff and volunteers to learn their jobs before they move into high gear. Sometimes personality conflicts arise among staff members or key volunteers which put a strain on the whole office. Other times volunteers only want to visit or they foul up everything they do. In such instances, it's better to let one or more of them go, the sooner the better for all concerned.

Don't be afraid to fire a volunteer. You can't afford to lose votes or other workers over one individual.

Deal with any staff crises swiftly and quietly, creating as few hurt feelings as possible. If you have a steering committee member who can handle this, it will save you many hours and much emotional energy drain.

Written job descriptions help staff members understand their responsibilities, although they must also be willing to do whatever has to be done. Sometimes volunteers or staff expect glamour and excitement, and are disappointed to find that most campaign work is repetitive and routine. (Two jobs you should not trust to volunteers: graphics and taping commercials. Be sure your advertising dollars are well spent—pay a professional to prepare your ads and brochures. Volunteers who work out of the office are hard to control, and if a volunteer comes up with something that's inappropriate or late, it's hard to do anything about it.)

After the race heats up and time starts running out, the campaign office vibrates and hums. Many campaign workers must stay on into the night, so be sure you include someone on your staff who has no deadlines to meet at home; a grueling campaign demands sacrifices from staff as well as the candidate.

Occasionally irresolvable differences occur between the candidate and her manager. If your manager leaves the campaign, turn your attention totally to bridging the gap. Enlist temporary help, if necessary, from any source you can to keep your campaign going. Find a replacement quickly and keep the internal dispute out of the paper and the gossip mill if you possibly can.

"The differences in management styles and perspectives for men and women...raise critical issues about the fit between managers and candidates," a recent study conducted by Greenberg-Lake* for EMILY's List concludes. "All candidates worry about management and good organization, but a well-run organization is even more important to women because of the role a strong organization plays in helping establish credibility. Women candidates turn over their managers more frequently than men, even in comparable races, and we found that these relationships remained somewhat unresolved for women candidates."

---

* Greenburg-Lake: The Analysis Group, Washington, D.C.

TIPS 36 - 45

Campaign Management

36

Design a top-notch written campaign plan. Find an experienced consultant or manager (paid or unpaid) to prepare a detailed plan for your approval at the start of your campaign. Include campaign strategy, theme, targets, fund-raising goals and methodology, major campaign events, time-lines showing important deadlines and planning and action points for campaign activities, organization, staff, and utilization of volunteers.

Stick with your basic campaign plan throughout the campaign. Switching strategies, unless mandated by poll results and competent advice, can fatally dissipate your efforts. Keep focused on campaign goals. Don't get side-tracked by what your opponent does or by "good ideas" your staff and supporters will want to try. Have a strategy ready to deal with negative campaigning if it comes (see tip 81).

If you are launching an all-volunteer campaign for a low-visibility race, buy three or four hours of a consultant's time to review your draft campaign plan and make suggestions. Even better, have that person meet with your kitchen cabinet to brainstorm your overall budget, analyze how you will win, and how to raise the money you need. Discuss the fee for this service in advance.

A campaign plan should include analysis of candidate and opponent strengths and weaknesses; polling strategy (identifying constituencies and their issues); the candidate's issues vis-a-vis her opponent and the electorate; a list of the major staff positions and their duties; the role and composition of the steering committee; three alternative budgets — optimistic, middle, and bare bones — with dates by which the money should be raised and spent; a fund-raising plan; major places the candidate should visit and when; strategies for gaining endorsements from various groups, debate/joint appearances, voter contact (including whether or not door-to-door canvassing and/or coffees will be utilized and why), editorial endorsement interviews, free publicity, and recruitment of volunteers. The plan should analyze the number of votes needed to win and show how those votes will be obtained.

Staff will usually include a campaign manager, fund-raising coordinator, press officer, scheduler, volunteer coordinator, bookkeeper (could be off-site), office manager, data base manager and possibly a driver-aide. Some of these positions might be combined or made part-time or volunteer. In any case, each position should have a written job description which lists job duties and supervision hierarchy. You as the candidate should personally hire the campaign manager and participate in hiring the scheduler and driver-aide because you will need to work closely with them.

You should also secure the services of a lawyer familiar with campaign election laws to serve as a volunteer campaign advisor and an accountant familiar with campaign reporting laws either to act as treasurer or to provide advice and direction to whoever does.

About a third of the way into the campaign, and again at the two-thirds point, schedule a "mid-course correction" conference with your campaign strategist and kitchen cabinet. While your campaign plan will be the bible you live by, it will need periodic reanalysis and reality check points.

37

Learn the business of campaigning as you would any other enterprise in which you have invested thousands of dollars. Attend campaign workshops. Study books on politics and campaigning (see appendix). Work on other campaigns at all levels. Talk to candidates and political pros experienced in a variety of campaigns.

Nothing beats preparation. This is true for hosting a dinner party, running in a marathon, excelling on a college exam, setting up your own business, or running a political campaign.

Men have studied the art of politics much longer than women. A 1987 reader survey conducted by *Campaigns and Elections* magazine found that 85% of its readership was male. Only recently have women campaign managers, consultants and strategists started coming into their own.

Consultants Foreman & Heidepriem of Washington, D.C. convened the first Campaign Women's Conference, a meeting of Democratic women campaign professionals which has grown significantly since its beginnings, in the winter of 1987. The group encourages more women to enter campaign management as a career. There is an ongoing need for trained and experienced women managers and for more people willing to go to other parts of the country to perform such campaign services.

The bipartisan National Women's Political Caucus has been in existence only since July 1971.* The League of Women Voters of the United States, which started the year women got the right to vote, 1920, has never opposed or supported candidates, focusing instead on the study of public issues. While many women gain public speaking experience and leadership training through their work in the League, candidates have to give up their visible League roles once they file for public office.

Ambition is the wellspring of politics, political scientists say, but it is opportunity which stirs that ambition. With opportunity for women candidates now greater than it has ever been, women must educate themselves in the art of campaigning to take advantage of this potential.

During election years, work for other candidates if you are not ready to run yourself. In non-elections years, make use of your library and inter-library loan resources to learn more about the political system and the lives of inspirational political figures of the past.

38

Allow enough lead time for preparation of activities and events, and details which precede them, such as drafts of solicitation letters, printing, etc. This is crucial! Use backward time tables with a master calendar posted where it can be seen and used. Check it every day. Utilize written guidelines and time check-lists for individual activities. Too many new-comers shift into high gear just as the campaign comes to an abrupt halt on election day.

A giant time chart should be posted prominently on the campaign office wall where everyone can see it. Every day for the five months preceding the election should have space for what will occur every hour in each of several categories: candidate, events, media, money, staff, volunteers, and committees. For example, a major fund-raising event would have entries for early staff and committee planning, obtaining volunteers for a mailing party and for follow-up phoning, solicitation of in-kind refreshments, writing press releases, preparation for the event itself, and attendance by the candidate and staff.

For a small campaign, side-by-side monthly planning calendar pages work well. Adhesive notes of different colors can be moved around for

---

* Founding spokespersons for the National Women's Political Caucus were Gloria Steinem, Bella Abzug, Shirley Chisholm, and Betty Friedan.

planning purposes with the candidate's business or personal commitments marked on the calendar in red.

Every campaign underestimates the time it takes to design and have finished materials printed. Candidates are often frantic because they don't have brochures to hand out and volunteers are calling for buttons and lawn signs. Mailings are held up waiting for flyers. Not starting soon enough on long-term projects is a standard campaign bugaboo. Press releases and fund-raising letters need to be carefully drafted and reviewed and approved and proof-read, all of which takes precious, calendar-eating time.

Buy a campaign manual for the office and be sure that those in charge of various campaign projects and events use the forms and timelines as a guide.

39

> *Be prepared for invisible campaign work to eat up chunks of time, for both you and your staff. Three-fourths of the tasks in a campaign are invisible to the public.*

There is never enough time in a contested campaign. On a "normal" job there's a bit of slack here and there to catch up on odd details or to sit down and think things over. In campaigns, there is no such luxury. Sometimes schedulers even forget that candidates need time to go to the bathroom, to change clothes or to drive from one part of town to the other.

One invisible time-eater is candidate issues research and study. Here again incumbents have the advantage—they work with the issues day after day and have full-time paid staff to develop positions as part of their paid government jobs. A woman candidate can't afford to be caught short without a good grounding in the issues, which may take her considerable time and study.

Your supporters may get nervous early in the campaign because they don't see anything happening in your race. This is when you are quietly raising money and burning the midnight oil on basic issues research. Staff is assembling lists and organizing committees and press kits and getting brochures printed and preparing mailing labels and planning events. (Inexperienced staff will think they have slack time when really there is none.) The media does little coverage until a couple of months before election day because the public is not interested. But these invisible details before filing deadline are essential to the smooth execution of the campaign's visible activity in the last month or two before the election.

Another greedy, invisible time-consumer is the telephone. Political consultant Cathy Allen advises that you put a three-minute egg timer on your desk and turn it over the minute you pick up the phone. Your goal is to get off the phone before you have to turn the timer over more than three times. Picture votes slipping through your fingers while you chat on and on and on.

40

Convert your knowledge of potential supporters onto a large computer base. Slow months between campaigns are an excellent time to compile lists of friends and potential contributors, to write down information about them you carry around in your head so it will be accessible to your staff. You may need professional assistance to design a top-notch computer system.

Campaign professionals suggest earmarking 10% of the campaign budget for computer equipment, lists, and programs. Only in the smallest or shortest campaign should a candidate shy away from utilizing the power and labor-saving potential of a computer. (The manual method would be card file systems.)

Because campaigns are only in business for a short time, they can't afford shake-down periods and experimentation or upgrading from one size computer to another in the midst of a campaign. You have to make a decision early and stick with it. Find a computer expert who understands political campaigns to advise you about both hardware and software. Try to get your computer set up before the campaign begins.

Some campaigns start with off-the-shelf database and word processing software programs and customize style sheets or formats for campaign purposes. Others buy campaign software programs and modify them to fit their needs. Be sure that whatever software you use comes with a good instruction manual. An inexpensive data base software program for under $150 is listed in the appendix. Some elected official you know may have developed campaign formats you could copy which run on commonly-used software. A volunteer may be willing to install your software as his or her contribution to your campaign.

Hire someone to input data, possibly part-time, so that when your campaign manager comes on board, he or she will have access to needed information.

Data elements and software capability you may wish to include in your system include volunteer lists with addresses, phone numbers, and names of spouses or "significant others"; contributors, receipts*, thank-you letters, and expenditure reports; potential contributor lists with prior donor histories; lawn sign locations; in-kind contributions and receipts; campaign committees; media contacts; lists of organizations which endorse. These software programs can be set up to sort by name, zip code, size of contribution, chronological order of contribution, occupation of donor, name of organization, etc.

You may also wish to use your computer for personalized "laser letters" scripted to target households, or to generate office forms, newsletters, and brochures designed with desk-top publishing software.

Don't try for a system big enough to collect and sort polling data or to generate canvassing lists for GOTV (Get-Out-The-Vote) efforts discussed in tips 59 and 60 unless you have expertise readily available to handle the job. The larger and more complex the systems, the more sophisticated your database manager and computer consultants will need to be.

---

* Know who was solicited to know who to thank, especially for major donors. Sometimes a businessman has his secretary sign his checks, or a woman gets furious if her spouse gets thanked in any way for *her* contribution. Ordinarily, however, your campaign receipts should be made out to the person who *signs* the check unless there's a note to the contrary attached. One candidate's guideline: have thank-you letters and envelopes addressed to *both* names, with the name of the check signer first (e.g., Martha & Frank Holiday, *not* Mr. & Mrs. Frank Holiday) if the check is drawn on a joint account. Put an asterisk by the name of the check-signer when the names are entered on your computer. Spouses who don't sign checks like to be thanked, too.

41

Delegate responsibility for scheduling your time to only one person. You will wish you could be in ten places at one time, but that can't be. In deciding which of those places to choose, your scheduler will need to apply campaign plan priorities and be able to say "no" diplomatically. (In a small campaign, the scheduler will be either the candidate or campaign manager.)

The scheduler will prepare your weekly schedule in detail, describing exactly where you are expected at what time, directions for getting there, who and what you'll find when you arrive. He or she may also need to arrange for drivers and aides to accompany you.

First priority on your schedule must go to fund-raising phone calls, appointments, and events; from 30% to 60% of your time should be devoted to this purpose. Criteria should be developed for the scheduler to use in making choices: for example, what size and type of audience is desirable; which target audiences does the candidate need most to reach for speaking engagements; which dates need to be kept open for contingency purposes; which geographical areas or organizations get precedence.

If you're employed full- or part-time in addition to your candidate duties, your scheduler will need to keep in close contact with you or your office regarding appointments during your regular work hours. An incumbent office holder may need a scheduling committee to work out conflicts between her job and the campaign.

Schedulers pursue speaking engagements for the candidate, investigate opportunities to debate the opponent, set up travel schedules and endorsement interviews. It helps if your scheduler knows your family and your personal habits.

If you are not satisfied with the kinds of places you're going or the way your appointments are handled, let your scheduler or campaign manager know. Usually in a medium to large campaign you won't be involved in scheduling decisions unless you have a personal request or preference. You will find it a relief to pass along invitations and requests to attend various functions and events for someone else to juggle.

Former campaign manager Patricia Soares of Rhode Island advises: "There are times during the campaign when the candidate has to do nothing and the family and staff have to allow her to do that. In a campaign you are kept on a seven-day-a-week schedule that sometimes goes for 12-16 consecutive hours. The candidate needs to take time out for herself. She needs quiet time."

Having someone else schedule your time will be one of the strangest experiences of your campaign. You sacrifice a good deal of personal independence in becoming a candidate. The scheduler you choose will need to exercise great care in allocating that most precious possession—your time. Choose that person well.

42

> *Know that most people wait to be asked before volunteering their services to a campaign. Folks need to know they are needed, and are more apt to say yes if asked to do something they would enjoy.*

You may be surprised who wants to do what—so don't limit people to any one thing when you ask. Let each person say his or her own yes or no, don't make that decision for them. Just be sure "no" is an acceptable answer to you—don't get your feelings hurt.

Have volunteer sign-up cards with boxes to check for specific tasks. When someone says, "Let me know what I can do," be sure the message gets passed on to staff.

Search for names of potential volunteers from rosters and committee lists of every organization to which you belong, as well as holiday card lists, business contacts, other friends and family. Make handwritten notations beside names of those most likely to respond for staff to contact later. Look over your contributor lists to see if there are names you've overlooked as possible volunteers.

Recruit a volunteer coordinator who will in turn find other volunteers from her own contacts as well as yours, and from new supporters neither of you have yet met. You may also need to enlist many key volunteers yourself. People are more apt to say yes to the candidate; the job carries more prestige that way. If people are busy the first time you ask, keep trying; ask for the best time weeks ahead and call them back.

Once you announce for office, you will be recruiting volunteers and seeking contributions everywhere you go. Have return envelopes ready to hand out for contributions and cards to fill out for volunteers. If there isn't time for that, make notations on their business cards or note paper to pass along to campaign staff. Your staff will enter the information on your computer master file so it can be accessed in various ways.

43

Demonstrate your appreciation of enthusiastic and committed volunteers; they can influence a race dramatically. Volunteers spread your message on a one-on-one basis and perform services which otherwise wouldn't get done or would cost money you do not have.

Make an extra effort to attend staff work parties, highlight volunteers' names in your newsletter, review lists of volunteers to thank when you see them, sign thank-you notes, make personal thank-you telephone calls, and consider issuing complimentary tickets to selected campaign events.

Many campaigns organize pizza feeds or light buffets for volunteers who take part in all-day door-to-door canvassing efforts during the last month of the campaign. This is a nice way to express appreciation for an important, tiring job, and your presence or that of a family member or campaign official for at least a few minutes will be appreciated. You can sometimes get food donated or at a reduced cost.

Be sure the work atmosphere at the campaign office is friendly and comfortable. Always have tasks available for volunteers to do and they will keep coming back.

44

Sign solicitation requests and thank-you letters to contributors and volunteers personally. Thank-you letters help build repeat contributors. Don't delegate this key contact with old supporters to others—save it for those late nights when you can't sleep.

Thank-you letters are a quick and efficient way to maintain personal contact with your supporters, and may be one of the few times during the campaign that you communicate personally with them. Thank-you letters can be preprinted, computer-generated, or typewritten, but should *always* be signed by the candidate, with a personal note added if possible. Don't handwrite your letters; you have higher priority ways to use your time.

A computer print-out which lists nicknames and spouses' names will be a great boon when writing personal notes. Names listed on envelopes may not be the ones you recognize and are often not the names your friends are accustomed to being called. Your memory for nicknames may blank out on you, too. You will be meeting a lot of new people.

For mass solicitation letters, add a personal P.S. to old friends if you have time, asking for a specific amount. It makes a difference when you ask personally and use their first names. Once a letter has been individualized, however, remember that it can no longer be sent by bulk mail and must be mailed first class.

45

Don't expect your campaign to run perfectly. "Organized chaos" is an apt description of any fiercely-fought contest. Nothing will be done exactly or as well as you might like. During a hectic campaign, miracles are required and time constraints are murderous. That's the nature of campaigns, part of their appeal. If possible, build leeway into your written campaign plan for missed deadlines and screw-ups.

Campaigns are whirlwind affairs. Then they're over.

One candidate put it this way: "There are loose ends everywhere. I'm an orderly person. I like to have filing systems, to know where things are, to be sure that the bills are paid, things are in repair, the snow tires get off the car. In sharing responsibilities at home and at the campaign, there isn't always someone to pick up the loose details, so some things are not taken care of. That's frustrating because I tend to be a perfectionist and you just can't be in a political campaign...."

If everything is getting done, you're probably not doing enough. No campaign is perfect, but if you and your staff give it your best shot, that's all anyone can ask. The best way to assure a smoothly-run campaign is to start early and be prepared when the crunch of the final two months hits.

A campaign is like starting up a small business, capitalizing it and creating a product once—then shutting down the whole operation.

TIPS 46 - 59

Candidate Obligations and Opportunities

46

Have a clear explanation of your motivation for running rehearsed and fluent. "Why are you running?" people will ask. Be prepared to answer cheerfully. Over and over again. Many people will be trying to make sense of you.

There's a fascination people have about why women run for office. With some questioners, they relay a sense of admiration and respect; others wonder with a frown on their face. Even though women in politics have come a long way, people still puzzle over why you would want to join the fray.

Voters don't want to hear that you're running, like others climb Mt. Everest, because it's there to do, or that it's your way of proving yourself as a human being. They don't want to hear a single-issue answer, either, such as women's rights.

Even supporters who are completely behind you on one issue will want to know that your concerns and focus are broader than that. They understand that you'll never get elected otherwise, and will not be effective on your one issue if you aren't versed in other areas as well.

Repeatedly the question will come: "Why are you running?" Even after you win, some will ask: "Why did you run?" Have a short answer, a medium-sized one, and a long, contemplative response prepared. Sometimes you can be more forthright than at others, but none of your answers should sound self-serving.

47

Learn public speaking. Enjoy it. Practice, practice, practice. Take public speaking lessons from a pro or join a Toastmasters Club to increase your effectiveness on the podium.

Audiences will judge you by your ability to articulate ideas and your forcefulness as a speaker. That doesn't mean giving up your personal style—it means learning how to look folks in the eye and to enunciate clearly and to paint pictures with your words.

Borrow or rent a camcorder to make video tapes of yourself giving speeches. Review them. Ask others to look at the tapes and ask how you could improve. Your body language may be even more important than your message

Eye contact is especially important. Find a couple of people in the audience who are intent on what you're saying, nodding their heads. Let your eyes take in the whole audience occasionally, then return to the two people who are nodding "yes." Nothing beats enthusiastic listeners to bring out your best as a speaker.

"Be sincere...be brief...be seated," said President Franklin Roosevelt in advice to his son.

Lighten up. Smile. Be relaxed. Tell a joke or two if you feel comfortable with that. Have a message that you believe in, and your sincerity will shine through. Show some personality. Nobody likes listening to a monotone talking head, or worse, a head that reads its speeches. At times you may need to read a preprinted major address or press statement, with copies given to the media. In that case; practice thoroughly ahead of time to make the reading natural. Be prepared for a wide variety of lecterns, podiums, microphones, and lack thereof, on the campaign trail.

All audiences want to be entertained as well as informed. There's always a bit of theater in every good speech. If you enjoy yourself in front of an audience, chances are your audience will enjoy themselves, too.

48

Find yourself a full-time driver-aide for a major race. Worrying about directions or whether you have brought the brochures and collecting names and addresses ought not be the responsibility of the candidate. Choose a driver-aide on the basis of compatibility and friendly demeanor.

At times you will need to rely on a series of volunteer drivers. But always travel with a helper to hand out literature and take down names and addresses as well as to find the destination on a map in advance and be sure you get there by the most direct route.

There are also safety reasons. "I was so wrapped up in the campaign that I once drove off from a gas station without having paid and with the gas nozzle still in the car," says Representative Lisa Naito of Portland. She did go back, of course, to square up, but the incident sold her on the need for a driver. Another safety reason: having a companion to walk with you to and from buildings you go to at night.

If your driver acts as a campaign aide, be sure he or she is cued into keeping you moving from one person to the next. It may be hard to wade right in and start shaking hands with everyone, so your aide can encourage people to seek you out. Some individuals will engage you in long conversations while other folks are standing around waiting to meet you. Your aide needs to tap you on the shoulder and move you on to other people.

In her first race for Secretary of State, when Norma Paulus became the first woman elected to statewide office in Oregon, she rode in a van with her campaign logo painted on the outside. Inside, she had a bunk to lie down on while someone else drove, covering the state from border to border. Other candidates do their own driving, even long distances, and end up exhausted from the strain and energy that demands. Driving is an important function that someone other than the candidate can best perform.

49

Be well prepared for your first joint appearance with your opponent; it will set the tone of the whole campaign. Rehearse carefully, have a speech written out (whether or not you actually follow it), and have staff ask you tough questions in a rehearsal session. Be rested and well dressed. If you have a male opponent, be prepared for one-upmanship based on non-verbal use of masculinity to connote power. Have responses ready for those who ask, "Why should I vote for you instead of your opponent?"

A psychological game between opponents kicks off the first time they appear together. Each candidate takes stock of the other, measuring their mettle and spirit. It sets a precedent for later occasions.

Joint appearances and debates are no longer the common denominator they once were in politics. Evaluate with your consultant or steering committee whether or not appearing with your opponent is in your best interest. It it is, push for it; if not, lie low.

Even if your opponent has an edge in public speaking skills, appearing with him will be to your advantage if his name familiarity is considerably higher than yours. Then you must actively seek such opportunities. Media exposure is too important to be missed, and often the media will cover only joint appearances. You can knock your male opponent for a loop by knowing your issues frontward and backward when you appear together.

The answer to why people should vote for you instead of your opponent needs to be positive. Say, "I am running to do...," or "for the reason that...." or "I am the only candidate in this race that...." Not, "I am running against so and so because...."

Your male opponent may try some subtle tactics to put you in your place. (Like "kick a little ass," only that wasn't subtle.) It may be his patronizing tone or over-deference, his calling you "my dear" or putting his arm around your shoulders, insisting that it's "ladies first" or sending his wife to take his place in scheduled joint appearances with you. Have a plan to combat this trend, one already tested on some male friends to be sure you don't sound hostile. Good humor works well.

50

Understand that you will need to be waited upon—an especially difficult lesson for women candidates, their families, and staffs to learn. You can't afford to spend your time doing things someone else could do for you. You will need to ask because others won't always remember to offer—partly because they're not used to performing personal services for women. Don't expect anyone to be your servant, or to do something you wouldn't or haven't done yourself.

Most men grew up being waited upon and take it for granted, while women usually had role models who considered others' needs first. Nor do women candidates have a wife at home to "soothe, feed, and comfort them, give gentle assurance, and do their laundry," as Carolyn Heilbrun puts it in *Writing a Woman's Life*.

A campaign is a collective effort with your election as the goal. Shake the habit of doing everything yourself. Make your need for assistance known. Consider organizing a network of friends to help with personal tasks. In her first race for the Oregon legislature in 1988, Representative Beverly Stein, a single woman, enlisted a support network of friends to pick up her dry cleaning, take her shoes in for repair, mow her lawn, and deliver a pot of soup to her house on a regular basis.

Providing of personal services can be especially sensitive for female staffers who associate it with the old tradition of women being the coffee-getters at the office. But personal tasks should be no different from the need for others to do the mailings and graphics and other campaign details. Keep reminding yourself to focus your time on things which only the candidate can do.

Make a special effort to be considerate of those who work closely with you. Sometimes in the rush and stress of a campaign, candidates remember to be charming to everyone else but those to whom they owe the most.

51

Notify the program director or master of ceremonies of your arrival at political functions, whether or not you are scheduled as a speaker. Office holders and candidates are often introduced or acknowledged at an event without advance warning. Don't assume that door greeters or others who see you will take care of this detail for you. Make the organization's leaders aware of your presence.

Candidates have to be seen and heard. It is the opposite of your childhood upbringing. Unless a list of candidates is being checked off at the door when you arrive, push yourself forward to find the master of ceremonies, the president of the organization, and the host and hostess, to let them all know who you are and that you are present. Think about the money it costs to buy name familiarity and consider this effort as saving dollars. Always wear a large name tag or campaign button or a permanent pin made by a local shop that clearly shows your name and the office you're running for.

You may be able to limit your time at an event to the crucial time when candidates are introduced. Always have your scheduler find out exactly when that will happen.

If you will be given time to speak, look around the audience to see who you know. Plan to weave their names into your remarks. "I see Joe Flannigan over there from Rockport; we used to work on the planning commission together." "Madeline Curry over on the other side of the room. I remember when she and I licked stamps together back in 1982...."

52

The best way to gather names and addresses and other offers of assistance while you're campaigning is to have an aide at your side or within beckoning distance to write things down and transfer that information to your computer files as soon as he or she gets back to the office. You and your staff should always carry note pads and/or volunteer sign-up cards along with return envelopes for campaign pledges.

Jimmy Carter describes, in his book *Why Not the Best?*, his dictating into a tape recorder while driving home from speaking appearances when he was preparing to run for Georgia governor—names, information about the community, speech notes for later use. The next day Rosalynn would write thank-you notes on an automatic typewriter which also recorded key information, including "code descriptions" of the people Jimmy had met.

Take advantage of the verbal offers of assistance you receive and keep track of the people you meet. That is how you broaden your support base, not just for this election, but for future ones, too.

53

The candidate's time needs to be budgeted as frugally as money, perhaps more. There's always the potential for a loan of more money, but never of more time.

In her book *In the Running*, Ruth Mandel discusses the difficulty women in various employment situations have finding time to campaign. Those who are economically independent with minimal family demands "are in the best position to find the time it takes to wage a viable political campaign," Mandel said. Being self-employed or working part-time or with a flexible schedule was next best. Hardest was to have primary household and family responsibilities and to work full time.

How much time you have available will make a considerable difference in your campaign plan. The campaign will have to adapt to your work and family demands at the same time that you must make every possible hour you can available to the campaign.

Don't assume that just because other candidates go door-to-door or attend coffees night after night that you need to do that, too. It all goes back to your campaign plan; it will tell you where you need to concentrate your efforts. Your scheduler will make the judgment calls to allocate your time according to your campaign plan criteria.

54

Be cautious about appearing anywhere with a male other than your spouse, campaign manager, or a campaign official. Always introduce whoever accompanies you and explain his or her responsibility to the campaign. If your spouse or a close male friend (if unmarried) rarely appears with you in public, you can expect rumors about any other man who travels with you. Your supporters will be uneasy if you are not sensitive to this issue—which is an especially difficult one for a single woman.

People have enormous curiosity about the personal lives of public figures. If a candidate shows up too often in the company of a member of the opposite sex, suspicious minds may jump to untoward conclusions, especially if you stop at a lounge for a drink on your way home. Political figures like Gary Hart and Wilbur Mills helped the public form impressions of politicians from which women are not immune.

Women have always had to worry about maintaining good reputations. Campaigning is no different from the rest of your life except that during a campaign you are in the public eye more often, in a veritable fish bowl.

"Women lobby differently (than men)," said Maryland Congresswoman Connie Morella as related in *Momentum: Women in Politics NOW*. "(Women) don't always have the opportunity for the kind of access that men have....a lot of lobbying took place at the Hilton Hotel (at the state legislature) at night over booze. Now a woman has got to be careful and she doesn't want to overbooze, and so there is that fine line...Most women, I think, do their lobbying through homework, through planning a strategy and then meeting one on one, and it might be a cup of coffee or it might be an early drink—but...(women) don't always have the free access in terms of reputation."

Female candidates should show up with their spouses, if married, as often as possible. Voters like to be reassured that a woman candidate's family supports her political aspirations, and a visible husband gives that appearance.

If you're not married, you may find curiosity about why you're single, although less so in today's world than yesterday's. A single woman who has never married may have a quiet whisper campaign started that she is a lesbian, which could hurt her chances of election in some areas. If you are single, have your steering committee and consultant consider this possibility and come up with a strategy to deal with it if it occurs. (Also see tips 81 and 93.)

55 *Assume that each new audience knows nothing about you or your race or the issues. What is boring repetition for you is information that each new audience needs to hear. Be careful of developing an "inside information" patter with your opponent or an interviewer that leaves your listeners in the dark. Address yourself to your audience, not the speaker's platform.*

Have a standard stump speech. If it works, stay with it. The biggest obstacle will be your own boredom. But you're not campaigning to entertain yourself; you are there to win votes. Expect to be bored. Stick with it.

Before your campaign shifts into high gear, prepare and rehearse three speeches: first, a 10-minute version explaining your qualifications, office sought, issues, and motivation, using word pictures and a couple of personal anecdotes; second, a three-minute abbreviation of the same; and third, a one-minute introduction for the times you barely get to pop your head up and sit back down again.

Opposing candidates who have previously debated issues may start their next confrontation where they left off, leaving at least part of their audience totally in the dark. Your opponent is not your audience; the people sitting out front and listening on the radio are. So forget your opponent is even present. Address yourself to the voters; your message is for them. Don't worry about repeating jokes over and over; go ahead and repeat them. Forget the campaign workers who've heard you a thousand times and could recite your speech for you. Concentrate on the undecided voter who is hearing you for the first time and needs to be persuaded that you are the best person for this job.

A woman manager who attended the second Democratic Campaign Women's Conference in the fall of 1988 said, "Everybody who ran a campaign knows that you're most successful when you're boring as hell, when, a month into the campaign—when a campaign staffer asks, 'What's our message?'—you can conduct, in chorus, whatever the phrase is.... The candidate will tell you he or she's tired of giving the same speech, and you tell them to give it again, because unless you give it 550,000 times, the message doesn't penetrate."

From the same conference: "Don't compromise the message, but do frame the message appropriately for the audience."

56

Clarify who can speak for you and who can't. A staff member or advisor may assume he or she knows your plans or stand on an issue, and cause erroneous news stories or rumors. Even your manager should speak only on issues you have discussed and agreed upon.

Reporters will talk to anyone who'll listen, and are not above putting words in people's mouths. Campaign workers must be warned not to talk to the press about the campaign. They shouldn't even talk about the campaign amongst themselves in public restrooms or elevators or walking down the street. Committee members and advisors should also be told exactly who the spokespersons are for the campaign.

Having a knowledgeable press officer is important. On a small campaign, this might be a volunteer or the campaign manager. A strong trust relationship needs to develop between the candidate and the person who writes press releases (and possibly speeches) and explains her positions to the media.

Press releases affect your basic credibility. No press release on issues—unless it rehashes those covered in prior written statements— should ever go out until you have approved it.

Generally speaking, the fewer people involved in communicating with the press, the better. Chances for contradictory statements from the campaign are thus reduced.

57

Find ego-boosters to keep your spirits up, to make you feel like a million dollars. While your self-confidence will get pumped up when dealing directly with voters, at other times you will feel like your nose is getting ground into the dust. Have someone ready to brush you off and set you back on your feet.

Things which can lift your spirits: a sincere compliment, a quiet hug, an infectious smile, the roar of a crowd. Some people have a knack for conveying optimism. Sit down with someone who thinks you're special when you need a dose of positive thinking. Your spouse or campaign manager may sometimes fill this role, but you will probably need other voices, too.

A new candidate is the center of probing attention. People listen to her thoughts and seek her opinions. "The intense focus on ME during the whole campaign was something different from anything I had ever experienced," one first-time candidate said.

Greeting voters one-on-one can pump up your ego. When you're on the phone every day trying to squeeze blood out of turnips, you can easily forget that you have fans out there eager to shake your hand.

In fact, you may need to learn to deal with adulation. When you're brought up more as a giver than as a receiver, as most women have been, it's not comfortable to have others admire you openly. It takes getting used to, like learning to receive a compliment graciously.

58

Smile. Relax. Be yourself. People like to see a candidate smile, and admire an irrepressible sense of humor. When you are feeling tense and brittle, use relaxation techniques. Concentrate on breathing deeply to oxygenate your blood. Try developing a "mantra" you can recite to yourself to help relax your muscles.

The most common complaint about individual women candidates is that they don't smile enough. Perhaps women still take this business of getting elected all too seriously. You need to be relaxed for smiles to come naturally.

You don't want a mannequin smile, though, or a smile that pops out at inappropriate times. What people enjoy seeing most is a genuine smile that says you like people and want them to like you.

Tone down the smiles on your official photograph if you're seeking a financial or judicial position. You don't want to look severe, but you do need to look like you mean business. In person, warm smiles are as important for judges, auditors, treasurers and comptrollers as for every other candidate.

59

Expect election day to be the longest day of your life. Waiting for a jury to come in, or expecting Santa as a child, is a comparable experience. Only those campaigns with a voter ID strategy will still be going at full speed on election day. Otherwise, relax, knowing it's up to the voters now. Go to an exercise or health club, go shopping, clean out the drawers of your desk, go to the beach or the mountains.

If your campaign has identified supportive voters and is mounting a get-out-the-vote (GOTV) effort on election day, your help and encouragement will probably be needed. In Tricia Smith's successful campaign for the Oregon Senate in 1990, she and other campaign workers identified solid "yes" votes for Smith on the doorstep and by phone throughout the campaign. These "yes" votes were computerized to be sure those voters got to the polls. (In most states, computerized "walking lists" can be purchased which list registered voters by street with party registration noted.)

At 3 p.m. on election day, Smith's poll-watching teams got together at headquarters with Smith there to energize them. Teams drove to every precinct and checked the poll books to find out which "yes" voters had not yet voted. From 5:30 to 7:30 p.m., volunteers, including Smith, phoned to remind those voters to get to the polls. Her margin of victory coincided almost exactly with the "yes" votes and follow-up GOTV targeting. Campaign manager Cherie Copeland said the candidate's election day involvement was a crucial part of that effort.

Some candidates and volunteers spend election day handing out brochures on street corners and displaying banners across major highway overpasses. But most voters have made up their minds by election day and a candidate with no voter ID strategy is usually justified in feeling that when election day dawns her work is done. Do your voting as soon as the polls open and spend the rest of the day as a free spirit.

An idea. It's nice to go out on the street and be around people when you aren't "performing" and when responsibility has passed from you to them. Visit the beauty shop for a hairdo; you will need to feel confident that you look good when election results start rolling in.

Once the polls close and your victory party—everyone calls them that, win or lose—gets going, you will be caught up in the excitement of watching returns on television and sharing war stories with constituents and supporters.

TIPS 60 - 71

Strategy

60

Calculate how many votes you will need to win and have a strategy for winning them, geographically and by methodology. **Target voters carefully, know what issues they're interested in, evaluate the costs of various strategies to reach them. Potential voters must be exposed to your name and message repeatedly. How many votes are needed? How will they be obtained?**

Winning can be reduced to mathematics. You have to get one more vote than your opponent to win. Your campaign plan should identify the number of votes you're going to need and where you're going to get them. If it doesn't, think this through with your kitchen cabinet or campaign manager.

Campaigns which identify "yes" votes and have a GOTV strategy for getting those voters to the polls usually keep an on-going tally as the campaign progresses. "Every commitment to your candidate is like a deposit in the bank," says former campaign manager Thalia Zepatos.

Reducing the game plan to numbers makes winning seem easier. In the primary, for example, you don't need half the voters, you only need half of the registered Democrats or Republicans who vote. (In crossover primary states, your calculations will be more complex.) Include consideration of the number of people who vote absentee and decide how you will reach them.

If several candidates are in the race, you could win with less than a third or a quarter of the vote. Polling will determine what percentage of votes are already in your column and identify themes that will sway undecided voters your way.* Most of your resources in the final three weeks should be aimed toward uncommitted voters.

---

* State senate candidate Judy Olson of South Dakota learned a lesson about reaching voters the hard way in the fall of 1990. A high-tech auto-dialing system she was using to contact people failed to shut down at 8:30 p.m. as it was supposed to, which she found out when she received a call from an irate voter at 3 a.m. She won anyway, earning a photo spot in *Newsweek* magazine.

61

Identify constituency groups which have a vested interest in who gets elected to your office. **Money, time, energy, printing presses, communications networks—all are potential resources available from these groups. Who stands to gain or lose by your election? What power does the office hold? What groups are affected personally, either at home or in the workplace, by the actions of the official you are seeking to become? Seek support from these sources.**

It's like that game of Monopoly—if you acquire Boardwalk and Park Place, along with monopolies on other key properties, you're sure to win. Gaining the support of key constituency groups should be a major focus of the campaign plan. The more groups you can reach, the broader your base becomes.

The kinds of questions that members of PAC boards may ask you include the following:

QUESTIONS FOR NEW CANDIDATES

1. What motivates you to run?
2. Why would you be a great person for this office?
3. What one thing would you like to accomplish in your first term?
4. Give three reasons why you will be a better candidate than your opponent(s).
5. What is the biggest issue facing your district?
6. How much will your race cost? How much did candidates in your race spend last time?
7. What is the voter registration in your district, by party, and what were the vote margins in your race (percentages) in the last two elections?
8. Do you have a strong campaign organization?
9. What are your major support bases?
10. How many hours a day are you spending on the phone raising money? How much have you raised so far?
11. Can you describe, in ordinary language, your strategy for winning the race?
12. When will you start walking precincts and how many hours a day will you spend meeting voters?
13. How will you overcome a woman's special need to prove her credibility and credentials?

Young professionals are a good source of support for women candidates, but figuring out how to reach them is not easy. And while labor is an old stand-by source for Democratic candidates, many of its leaders are still uncomfortable supporting women.

Don't overlook churches and synagogues. In many cities, for example, black ministers are particularly powerful and active in politics, introducing favored candidates from their pulpits on Sunday mornings. (Washington, D.C. Mayor Sharon Pratt Dixon was elected without the support of the ministerial coalition, however.) Since churches are a classic example of male hierarchy, women candidates may face built-in bias here, too. But if churches in your area do introductions, by all means take advantage of that opportunity.

Various ethnic and special interest groups make endorsements and rally around candidates. Hispanic groups are becoming active across the country. Most large cities have black and "rainbow" (coalitions built for Jesse Jackson's candidacy) caucuses; Greek communities were a ready-made base of support for Michael Dukakis. Members of your own church or synagogue should not be neglected as a potential source for contributions of time and money.

Endorsements, volunteers, money—all can flow from groups which are convinced that your election will make a difference in their lives. Identify your friends and foes. The same kinds of resources may be put on the line against you from the other side.

62

Do polling in every major race. Polling is invaluable for pinpointing constituencies, targeting audiences, defining strengths and strategies. But don't let polls mold or warp your opinions. You may need your own version to counter your opponent's data and possibly that of the media.

Basically, you want to know: How many people will vote for me? What percentage of people know my name? Polling questions are asked of a cross section of voters to obtain a spread of age, gender, party, geographic area and occupation, in proportion to the total population.

Benchmark polls, in-depth surveys to help develop campaign strategy, are normally conducted a year to six months before an election. They will also give you numbers (name familiarity and who's ahead) with which to measure trends, so that shifts in voter opinion and image can be tracked. Later polls should be able to tell you if your message and theme are getting across to the voters.

If your budget does not allow as much polling as you'd like, consider piggy-backing on another poll for basic name familiarity and "who's ahead" data. A rule of thumb is to spend 5% to 10% of your budget on polling and voter research. Explore the possibility of pooling resources with candidates for other offices in your district and sharing information. Find out if a group favorable to your candidacy is doing a poll which they would share with you, or seek an organizational sponsor to pick up the cost of doing a poll as an in-kind contribution to your campaign.

The fewer dollars you have, the more important it is to spend them strategically. Polling will help you do that. Once you have a poll, use it. There's no point in spending the resources unless you put the results to work in your campaign.

"Push questions" which ask voters negative things about your opponent and positive things about yourself can border on unethical campaign practices if not used fairly. False information can be inserted in the following otherwise legitimate question: "Now, if you learned (negative facts about your opponent learned through research of his record), would this make you more or less likely to vote for him, or make no difference?"

In telemarketing campaigns, "voter persuasion" callers—whose purpose is to sway the voter rather than seek their opinion— pretend to be pollsters and pose negatives about a candidate which aren't true. Such calls not only are unethical, but may violate state laws. If such call are used against you, contact your lawyer and strategist at once to find out what actions can be taken.

In a legitimate in-depth poll, push questions are needed to learn what issues and attitudes would change voters' minds. They are a good way to explore ways to defuse potential negatives in your own record.

If you have an abundance of workers and little money, a do-it-yourself polling methodology is available—assuming that time allows, that volunteers are reliable, that your volunteers can put in structured hours, and that you can control the quality of the work done.* (See *Public Opinion Polling*, by Celinda Lake, in the appendix.)

---

* The U.S. Commerce Department also sells to the public, through NTIS (National Technical Information Service), a software program first developed for use by the General Accounting Office (GAO) which allows individuals to conduct interviews or surveys by phone, by providing the caller with questions to ask and allowing instantaneous entry of responses. Ordering information for this software, manuals, and a demonstration disk is included in the appendix.

Caution is in order. Someone skilled needs to draft appropriate questions, and not everyone makes a good interviewer. Volunteers have to be trained and supervised. Not every state has lists of registered voters with names, addresses and phone numbers. This kind of project eats up copious amounts of valuable time and volunteer resources which may be needed for other things. Don't start it if you can't finish it. You may also be misled by your results if valid statistical samples were not drawn.

63

Be prepared to deal with gender as a factor in political races for the foreseeable future. Probing voter attitudes about gender will help you know what to expect and how to counter skepticism about your capabilities. Enlist the aid of someone experienced in framing polling questions to make the best use of the information you gather.

The higher the office sought, the more gender becomes a factor in political campaigns. If a substantial number of women are already in office in your community, gender will make less difference to the voters. Barriers have dropped the most in volunteer and lower-paid positions (surprise!).

The seven Texas women elected mayors (recent or current) of the ten largest cities in Texas were profiled in August 1990 *McCall's* magazine. "There will never be another time when a woman's ability to serve in the public sector will be questioned simply because she is a woman," Mayor Kathy Whitmire of Houston is quoted as saying. Mayor Lila Cockrell of San Antonio said the struggle for acceptance by women in public life at the municipal level was over, "but when you look at the composition of the Legislature and the Congress, you know we still have a long way to go." However, only one of the seven women mayors, Kathy Whitmire of Houston, received what the article termed an "executive salary."

When Liz Holtzman ran for district attorney of Kings County (Brooklyn) New York in 1981, people on the street said to her, "Liz, I voted for you for Congress, I voted for you for Senate, but D.A., that's not a job for a woman.* How can you cope with the pressure? How can you

---

* Liz Holtzman became a national figure in her first term as a Congresswoman in 1974 through her aggressive questioning during President Nixon's impeachment hearings. She gave up her Congressional seat to run unsuccessfully against an incumbent U.S. Senator in 1980. She served as Kings County D.A. until elected in 1989 as New York City Comptroller.

deal with so many men working under you? How can you stand up to criminals?"

Find out through polling how much difference gender makes to the voters in your area. A significant gender gap occurred in voting patterns for the 1990 gubernatorial races of Ann Richards in Texas, Dianne Feinstein in California and Barbara Roberts in Oregon; all three received 16% more female votes than male.

If you end up in a race against a female candidate, don't worry about it unless you're concerned about splitting support bases as discussed in tip 77. Women facing women is bound to happen with increasing frequency as the number of female candidates continues to climb. Just don't allow the male political structure to identify token "women's seats" that all female candidates are pushed toward.

64

View gaining name familiarity and raising money as your main campaign goals. Political neophytes almost always have an inflated notion of their name recognition and grossly underestimate the time and money needed to change that. The cause-effect relationship between incumbency, name familiarity,* and money (the three top indicators of a winning race) creates a tough circle to break.

As a first-time candidate, name familiarity will be a major hurdle. Issues, gender, qualifications, credibility, a warm smile, a well-organized campaign—none of those will matter if the voters haven't heard of you. (The exception is running against an office holder with whom voters are so disgusted that anyone with an organized campaign could win—in which case your main task is to keep other candidates out so you don't split the anti-incumbent vote.)

It takes money and media exposure to increase your name familiarity. An advertising rule of thumb is that voters must be exposed to your name at least three times (some authorities say seven) before it has an impact. One mailer to a household isn't going to do it.

---

* Once elected, you need to maintain your name familiarity. Have your receptionist answer the phone, "County Clerk Sharon Mitchell's office." Make public appearances. Visit with the editors of your local newspaper. Be sure your name is prominently displayed on the cover of reports issued by agencies you supervise. This is not self-aggrandizement. Your constituents want to know what the person they elected is doing. Unlike a single boss, your public stockholders won't remember your name unless you remind them.

One problem unique to women political candidates is that most married women's names are hidden behind their husband's names on vendor and organization records, on mail boxes, on return address stamps, in phone books.* This is usually true even if the woman retains her own last name after marriage.

In a judicial contest, none of the candidates, even the incumbent, is usually well known. Judicial candidates rely on traditional campaign methods—direct mail, radio, newspaper ads, etc.—for name familiarity. Photos are especially important in such races so the voters can see for themselves that you look stable, reliable, trustworthy.

Oregon State Senator Betty Roberts (no relation to Barbara) used name familiarity gained in a previous statewide race as ammunition to convince a Republican governor to appoint her (a Democrat) as the first woman Oregon Supreme Court Judge in 1982. She informed the Governor and press that she would run whether or not appointed. The Governor gave in gracefully.

Sometimes judges are allowed to insert the word "incumbent" after their names on the ballot, whether previously elected or appointed. The Oregon legislature abolished candidate ballot slogans as an economy measure in 1983, but two years later passed an exception for judges. It is a powerful tool for incumbent judges and a formidable hurdle for challengers.

---

* Phone companies in twenty states allow dual phone book listings without additional cost for two persons with the same surname residing at the same address. Such listings have to be requested; they are not offered automatically. Other states charge an initial changeover fee of around $5 or an ongoing fee ranging from 25 cents to $2 per month for including a second name in the telephone director. (1989 Annual Report of the National Association of Regulatory Utility Commissioners.)

65

Think of that Monopoly game again. You'll be playing a similar contest call Endorsements, pitted against your opponents, for the entire campaign. Unlike the board game, however, you will have no idea, starting out, how many endorsements there are to collect or what kinds of resources you will need to acquire them. How valuable are they, what purpose do they serve? Where do you find out? And how convince the banker that you're the winner in this game?

Seeking endorsements drains an enormous amount of candidate and staff time, more than you can imagine. Endorsements from organizations often involve lengthy questionnaires which require considerable research, extensive interview processes, and hours of lobbying key players by candidates and their supporters.

Early endorsements from respected elected officials and community leaders are gained chiefly through personal contacts and lobbying. These individual endorsements (especially male ones) can help give you the status and credibility you need to convince other groups and individuals, including newspapers, to support you. (A possible polling question: "Rate the following community leaders: Whose opinion would you value most highly?")

Your opponent will be fighting for the major endorsements, too, and if you don't put forth a good effort, the prizes will go to him by default. But choose which endorsements to seek. Don't assume that you have to go after every one.

In filling out lengthy surveys, ask a friendly elected official to share the answers he or she has given that organization in prior years to give you a starting point. A staff member or volunteer could draft answers for you, but insist on seeing draft questionnaires before they're finalized. You will have to defend your answers.

66

Realize that your advertising agency can make or break your campaign. Be sure that your image, as portrayed by your advertising agency, is faithful to you and your campaign plan. Preview ads with your pollster and kitchen cabinet (or steering committee) present. The extent of an ad agency's involvement in campaign planning, strategy, and issues needs to be negotiated in advance.

Many advertising agencies don't understand political advertising; many won't touch it. Don't wait long to look for the agency that can best represent your needs. Find out what candidates the agency has represented in the past and whether or not those candidates were satisfied. Usually there is no cost to the campaign for an advertising agency's services unless they do extra work, such as graphics design. Ad agencies get a commission from the media for all the advertising they place.

The line between various kinds of consultants—pollsters, advertising agencies, and strategists—has become increasingly blurred in recent years. One firm might do all three parts, but most firms aren't set up that way. Therefore, the components must be integrated either by designating one consultant as coordinator or having your campaign manager call them together to share information and ideas. Your campaign manager will need to monitor your advertising agency to be sure it is targeting the right audiences with the message your polling and strategy demand.

67

Focus scarce advertising dollars on complete penetration by one or two media rather than trying to do everything. You'll receive all kinds of advice from your supporters about advertising because this is the part of the campaign they see. Television, radio, direct mail, post card campaigns, leafleting, billboards, lawn signs, newspaper ads, satellite offices, door-to-door canvassing, telephone campaigns, sky-writing, helium balloons and other imaginative things all have their strengths and uses in different campaigns.

Use each medium deeply enough to penetrate your constituency before adding a new medium. Production overhead is very costly and takes away from voter contact, so every new medium has an overhead factor to consider. Decide where you're going to concentrate ahead of time and have alternate budget packages planned so you can eliminate an advertising component if money does not come in.

Many campaigns try to do too many things without the resources to do them well. Your friends and supporters will say, "How can you win without TV? Where are your lawn signs?"

You can't do everything. Stay with your plan.

68

Find one low-cost piece of campaign paraphernalia (Buttons? Bumper stickers? Window decals?) plus a brochure, for mass production. Don't let paid consultants or staff overrule some concession to time-honored campaign symbols and the desire your volunteers have to display such emblems proudly.

Your supporters need a visible memento to advertise their commitment to you. Keep it simple and inexpensive, and stick to one item (in addition to a simple brochure) for most races. The choice will depend on the size of your district and the needs of your race. Remember that every dollar spent here is a dollar not available for advertising.

Do have something. You can't go empty-handed to a candidate fair or a coffee or an endorsement meeting. People want an item they can look at and hold in their hands that says your name. A simple but efficient handout is a campaign business card. Print them with your name, office sought, and logo, plus the address and phone number of your campaign office and campaign manager. If it is your only handout, consider printing your photo, name and office sought on the other side of the cards.

Because anything of value might be seen as buying votes, many state laws limit what you can give voters. Check with your local elections division before ordering any voter handout other than a business card or brochure.

69

Count on party support and that of other office holders in your party once nominated in a partisan primary. It won't come running, you'll probably have to chase it and pin it down.

The old boy network of partisan politics may still exclude women if you don't elbow your way in and insist on equal treatment. You may not want the support of all party *candidates*, though; seek the help of those who are credible and successful, and whose positions on specific issues are acceptable to your constituents. (Be prepared to return the favor later.)

Usually, Republican candidates receive more financial support from their party than do Democrats. In 1986, the Republican party raised five times as much as the Democratic party. The Republican party also offers, depending on the state, sophisticated services such as computer software and training, which is not as available to Democratic candidates. If you become the Democratic or Republican nominee in a legislative race, your party's legislative caucuses may help you if your race looks promising.

Candidates in a partisan race have an advantage over nonpartisan ones, such as judicial and many municipal offices, because an "extended family" of political party members is usually waiting to offer support once you've earned the nomination of the party.

Party allegiance is stronger in some states than others. Both Alaska and Connecticut showed streaks of independence in 1990 by electing Walter Hickel and Lowell Weicker as their governors, both without their former Republican labels. Unless you have the name familiarity of a Weicker or Hickel, however, if you want to get elected, your best chance is to run either as a Republican or Democrat. Independents and third party candidates may articulate issues which need to be aired, but they rarely get elected.

In recent years, the Republican position on abortion rights has alienated many young women. However, there are many Republican women working actively for a woman's right to choose. Congresswoman Olympia Snowe of Maine has co-chaired for many years, along with Colorado Representative Pat Schroeder, the Congressional Caucus for Women's Issues. Liberals and conservatives coexist in the women's caucus, Representative Snowe told a *New York Times* reporter, "because on social issues, on women's issues, we all tend to be in the center."

There are people who vote for the party nominee, regardless. Democratic candidate Lisa Naito found this out when she introduced herself on the doorstep as a former county prosecutor. The woman of the house looked puzzled. She thought Lisa said former *prostitute*. When the woman finally understood that Naito had worked for the district attorney's office, the woman said, "That's okay, I was going to vote for you anyway. I'm a registered Democrat."

70

Avoid endorsing any other candidate when you are in a close race; you don't need anyone else's baggage. Nor should you seek endorsements from candidates who are themselves in contested races. The head of your party ticket who is very popular would be an exception to this rule.

If you decide you must endorse a candidate you don't like or with whom you disagree on basic issues, do it with as little fuss and involvement as possible.

In the 1990 fall elections, Marjorie Clapprood of Massachusetts was teamed on the Democratic ticket as Lt. Governor with John Silber running as Governor. Silber managed to offend and alienate everyone. "She (Marjorie Clapprood) was running with someone who epitomized everything she worked against," said a spokesperson for the Coalition for Lesbian and Gay Civil Rights which endorsed conservative William Weld as the lesser of two evils. An article in the *Boston Globe* after the loss of her ticket said, "Of all the Democrats sent packing this fall, Clapprood has perhaps the most promising future." Some observers say she paid a heavy price for teaming up with Silber and standing by him in several campaign controversies, losing much of her core support along the way. Clapprood has been called flamboyant, outrageous, irreverent. It will be interesting to see if she is able to shed her association with Silber in the future.

If you have a choice in the matter, the general rule is: Put your own race first and don't get dragged into the campaigns of others.

71

Be prepared for difficult and constant scheduling and cancelling choices. Written criteria will help your scheduler evaluate the relative merits of various appearances, and avoid filling your calendar too early.

Final scheduling decisions will ordinarily be made by your scheduler or campaign manager, but you will need to justify these selections to others. (See tip 41.) Balance is needed between keeping engagements you have committed to and the broader goal of winning the election.

Your opponent will sometimes cancel out on scheduled joint appearances that you've spent a lot of time preparing for. If that happens, try to find a way to use his or her absence to your advantage. Certainly it will not earn him any points with the audience. If your opponent ducks out frequently, let the voters know about it.

When a change is required for a scheduled appearance, having talented and well-known surrogate speakers ready to appear on your behalf on short notice will help soothe those you have to disappoint.

TIPS 72 - 76

Issues

72

To get elected, it matters *how* you say it more than *what* you say. People vote for candidates based on many reasons, in somewhere near the following order:

- NAME FAMILIARITY
- TRUST
- INCUMBENCY
- PERSONALITY AND STYLE
- AGAINST OPPONENT'S ISSUE OR RECORD
- CANDIDATE'S ISSUES
- PARTY AFFILIATION
- QUALIFICATIONS

When both candidates' names are well-known, name familiarity ceases to be a factor. Newspaper endorsements are less important then, too, because voters make up their minds based on media images. Some researchers say voters develop strong opinions by *watching* the candidates on television, *without hearing* what they say.

"Feelings are three or four times as important as issues or party identification (in selecting a president)," said Yale psychologist Robert Abelson as quoted by *Time* magazine. If a candidate pushes the hope and pride buttons and avoids touching the anger and fear buttons, Abelson said, he or she will probably win.

George Bush did a masterful job of pushing the American hot buttons of optimism and patriotism during the Persian Gulf War, themes previously used successfully by FDR and Reagan. As Peggy Noonan relates in *What I Saw at the Revolution*, when she first started speechwriting for President Reagan she was told, "It always has to be positive with him (Reagan). Never 'I'll never forget,' always 'I'll always remember.'" An important lesson in the power of simple words.

Mayoral candidate Sharon Pratt Dixon carried a broom—and on election night held high a shovel—as symbols of her intent to clean house after Washington, D.C. residents had been subjected to months of unsavory publicity about backroom politics and drugs. She had inspired the voters' trust. *The Washington Post* quoted this first black woman to head a major city as urging D.C. residents in her January 1991 inaugural address to create a "city of hope, humanity, and excellence."

Emotions aren't the only thing which sway voters, of course. Issues and qualifications play a significant role, but more as a way to gain credibility and trust than for themselves. Again, *how* you talk about an issue, your persuasive power, makes the difference. You've got to look like you know what you're talking about, and that you are competent and compassionate. "Tough and caring" was the apt theme Dianne Feinstein used in 1990 which brought her within inches of the California governor's chair.

If you live in a state which allows slogans on the ballot, make the word DEMOCRAT or REPUBLICAN the first word of your slogan in any election in which your party has the voter edge. If you are an incumbent, put the word REELECT or RETAIN first. Some voters won't think any further once they see those trigger words.

73

Research campaign issues personally if you possibly can; you must be credible on the issues. Early in the campaign, identify, select, and define topic areas which can be tied to your prior experience and developed into examples that audiences will understand. Expect to receive briefings from volunteer researchers, review written drafts of short and long versions of issue papers, and participate in practice sessions in which you respond to hypothetical questions.

Male political consultants say a candidate has only two roles during a campaign—raising money and meeting voters. A woman candidate has a third role, though: preparing herself to be an authority, an expert, on major issues which arise during the campaign as well as two or three issues she can claim for her own. These issues will be the core of the campaign for you; they will reflect your passion for the job you seek.

Men are more comfortable using talk to claim attention than are women, Deborah Tannen notes in her best-selling book, *You Just Don't Understand*. Women who are talkative at home, for example, seldom speak up in public meetings. Tannen herself is very comfortable on radio and television talk shows because she is there in the role of *invited expert*. "When I am a guest, my position of authority is granted before I begin to speak," Tannen says. She doesn't call in to talk shows, however, because she'd have to establish her credibility first by explaining who she is (which women don't do because it's tooting their own horn.) For the same reason, she rarely asks questions from the audience following a lecture. Does this sound familiar?

To gain needed self-confidence, women need to feel qualified, to be an expert, an authority. Most first-time candidates and women seeking higher office will need to take extra time to learn issues related to the job they seek.

74

Pick two or three major issues and stick with them; learn them frontward and backward and upside down. Your issues must have sufficient scope and depth, and broad public appeal. In-depth polling can help identify what relevant issues are of current concern.

Restricting your campaign to two or three major issues will be frustrating, but it must be done. The principle for containing your issues is the same as for concentrating media dollars and for developing one basic stump speech and sticking to it.

Find issues beyond the traditional ones women have always been associated with; voters will take for granted that you know social issues and will not give you the same credit for promoting them as they would a male candidate. Develop an economic issue, an environmental one, one on law and order.

Congresswoman Barbara Boxer of California gained the title of "Pentagon Watchdog" through revelations of $7,600 coffee pots and $400 hammers in military procurement practices. Boxer, first elected in 1982, has consistently received high marks from the League of Conservation Voters for her strong environmental record. She positioned herself early for a U.S. Senate race in 1992.

Women also need to emphasize issues which will demonstrate their managerial and financial expertise. Voters have a stereotypical image of men as automatically being more qualified in these areas. The issues you develop need to tie-in to your overall campaign theme and the slogan used on your brochures and in campaign literature.

As important as issues are, however, always remember that they are more a showcase for your style than for any particular issue or solution. The way you present your arguments and proposals will demonstrate to the public how you approach problems and will reveal your basic values. Issues are the tool by which you display your potential, and seldom will any one issue win or lose a race for you.

75

Avoid getting side-tracked into debating topics unrelated to your office. **Learn to divert questions to the issues on which you want to focus. Recognize that every issue is more complex than it appears at first blush. Stay out of controversial issues which have nothing to do with your race, especially if you don't know the pros and cons of the debate well.**

Pick your fights carefully, as the political axiom goes. Decide which issues you will be involved in, and don't try to cover the waterfront. On the other hand, you don't want to appear wishy-washy by ducking controversy. Learn to turn the agenda toward your topics or simply be a good listener. If undecided, explain that you have not yet had a chance to fully research the issue, that you see good points on both sides and will make up your mind when you have all the facts.

Even though issues don't rate high on the list of reasons voters vote for candidates, in a tight race, issues can play a deciding role. Note this example of the wrong way to use issues: Near the end of a heated battle to retain her seat, former Portland City Commissioner Margaret Strachan called a press conference to bring up, unconnected to anything else going on at the time, the Hanford nuclear waste dump in southeastern Washington. The issue gained her no votes that she didn't already have and may have alienated voters by giving Hanford precedence over city issues. While she was talking about nuclear waste, her opponent was posing solutions to deal with neighborhood crime, the number one issue on voters' minds. Strachan lost, partly because voters felt her opponent was more in tune with their needs than she.

The position you run for will help determine which issues you should side-step and which ones you can't. For example, a candidate for county elections director would stay out of the abortion issue, but a state legislative candidate who tried to duck it would be pilloried for waffling.

Judicial codes of ethics ordinarily prohibit candidates for judgeships from stating their positions on issues. Any political activity that "creates a reasonable doubt about a judge's impartiality toward persons, organizations or factual issues that forseeably may come before the court on which the judge serves," is usually forbidden.

A candidate for a municipal position which carries quasi-judicial responsibilities must also be careful not to compromise herself on matters which might come before her after she is in office.

76

Carefully investigate tips about unethical or illegal activities by your opponent and handle them like a time bomb. As the candidate, you should refrain from making any charges. You and your manager may decide to give information about your opponent to a newspaper or a watchdog organization for follow-up, or to forget the whole thing as too risky to handle. Negative campaigning can quickly backfire, especially for women candidates.

"The hardest thing about any political campaign is how to win without proving that you are unworthy of winning."   — Adlai Stevenson

A woman candidate is advised to be extra cautious about using negative tactics because it may destroy the perception voters have that she is not the usual politician and that she is above or outside the traditional "slime" of politics.

Negative campaigning can backfire. Minnesota Republican U.S. Senator Rudy Boschwitz committed a major gaffe in questioning the religious convictions of challenger Paul Wellstone, a fellow Jew, and the non-Jewish manner in which Wellstone had raised his children. Observers also credited Boschwitz's overconfidence and Wellstone's witty TV commercials for Wellstone's 1990 upset. One ad* titled "Looking for Rudy" was a take-off on the movie "Roger and Me," and showed Wellstone searching the state for his opponent to debate with him. The ad aired only three times on paid TV, but created such interest that the free media played it, too.

---

* A videotape including this commercial and others is available as "The Best of 1990" which can be ordered through *Campaign* magazine, see appendix.

It is important to draw a distinction between *misrepresentation* of an opponent's record versus exposing and attacking an opponent's *true record*. Some candidates are able to win without discussing their opponents (a strategist should advise you on this based on poll results), but if your race is against an incumbent, exposing and attacking his or her record is almost a given, particularly if your race covers a large district, one which you can't personally reach door-to-door. (The advantages of running against a "bad guy" are discussed in tip 78, how to deal with negative charges made *against* you in tips 81 and 87, and the importance of researching your own record in tip 93.)

The law treats candidates who seek the limelight as "public figures," so you can't be held liable for defaming your opponent if you believe what you say about him to be true.* In addition to the tort of defamation, however, seven states provide a remedy to the candidate who loses an election if statements printed by his or her opponent's campaign can be proven false. Oregon's law says that if a court of law finds that a false printed statement made deliberately by a winning candidate reversed the outcome of an election other than for the state legislature, then that office is declared vacant.

Implying moral turpitude or questioning someone's honesty and honor also tread on dangerous grounds, but true facts about your opponent's record are fair game: stands on issues, management experience, attendance record at meetings, not representing the needs of the district, not listening, ignoring the voters between campaigns, being out of touch with the voters, votes on bills, bills sponsored and not sponsored, votes in committees, absences when votes were taken, reversals of positions. *How* you portray that record is the part which can get into "negative" campaigning.

The timing of your broadside also makes a difference. Late in the campaign, your charges may be dismissed as a desperate attempt by a losing candidate to grasp at straws or as part of the campaign silly season. The media may also chastise you for waiting too long.

---

* In *Vanasco vs. Schwartz*, the U.S. Supreme Court held in 1975 that the "actual malice" standard applicable to public figures covers campaign speech, according to *State Legislatures* magazine. Graham Johnson, executive director for the Washington State Public Disclosure Commission, is quoted as saying, "The circumstances of campaigns are unique and not well-documented, and proving malicious intent on the part of a candidate is an almost insurmountable task." Some legislators are trying to curb negative campaigning through fair campaign practice codes and other proposals.

If your resources are limited, however, like those of Joan Kelly Horn who did not have enough dollars to sustain a lengthy exposure period or to run "positive" ads (her opponent outspent her 2 to 1) you may need to wait until late in the campaign when the voters are paying closer attention.

"Horn used a late-breaking, all-or-nothing blitz of negative television commercials questioning Buechner's integrity," said political reporter Mark Schlinkmann of the *St. Louis (Missouri) Post Dispatch* shortly after Horn's upset victory over incumbent Congressman Jack Buechner by a 54-vote edge. "The ads likened Buechner to a pig at the public trough and cited suits filed against him involving his business dealings and a trip taken with his girlfriend to Paris."

"Jack Buechner junkets, leads parades, appears on TV and self promotes," said a Horn for Congress issues handout. "What he does not do is work for the District or the area. He comes late to issues—whether toxic waste disposal or airport expansion—or sits on the fence."

In a tough re-election race in Washington state which she won handily, incumbent Congresswoman Jolene Unsoeld decided to "go negative" on her opponent three months before the 1990 election. Pollster Tim Hibbitts described her successful tactics this way, "She very effectively defined him to the point that the voters decided they preferred to go with the devil they did know to the devil they didn't."

TIPS 77 - 81

Opponents

77

Keep your strongest opponents out of the race by any means possible within ethical and legal constraints. This is a time-honored, but controversial, strategy. While you may need a contested primary to gain name familiarity, a bruising contest will devour your financial and emotional resources. The most effective way to deter potential opponents is to have money in the bank and support already lined up.

A method successfully used by male candidates against potential female opponents is for acquaintances to call her to say how much more effective the male candidate would be in that position than she. Since there is a built-in stereotype, even in women's minds, that a man will succeed where a woman won't, this tactic discourages all but the most determined female candidates.

If you are a viable candidate who gets several unsolicited calls or letters of advice from someone other than a trusted friend or advisor, it may be part of a planned strategy to keep you out of a race. You should be flattered that you are considered an opponent worth trying to frighten off, but not deterred by this pressure. Base your decision on whether or not this is the right race, the right time, and whether or not you could win.

If you are serious about running and the candidate pressuring you is someone who shares your political philosophy and support bases, the two of you or your representatives should sit down together to discuss the possibility of a third candidate defeating you both. Whether you can work out an amiable solution is debatable, but most of your potential supporters will sincerely hope that the two of you can either agree to a coin toss or to enter binding arbitration adjudicated by someone you both trust. However, resolution must come before either of you fully activates a campaign.

Be aware, if you are considering trying to preempt someone from entering a race, that such tactics can backfire and push a teetering candidate *into* the race instead of out. To some, being told that another person would be a better candidate or elected official is waving a red flag. Emotions and ego usually get in the way of reason.

When Congresswoman Rosa DeLauro decided to run for Congress from Connecticut's Third District in 1990, she followed her own advice as former executive director of EMILY's List and made fund raising her top priority. She scared away her primary competition by raising $100,000 a year before the election, and by getting early support from people on town committees, closing that support off to other potential opponents.

78

Understand that running against a "bad guy" is easier and more rewarding than against one who is perceived as a "nice guy." If you represent a different philosophy from your opponent, and take opposite positions, your supporters will be more motivated to contribute their time and money to your race. You compete against other races for a major portion of your resources.

Know who you are running against—their family, civic, volunteer, church or synagogue and elective backgrounds. What are their strengths, weaknesses, supporters, finances? Are they honorable or sleezes? What can you anticipate from them? Take all these factors into account in your planning.

The hardest race to run is against a "nice guy" or "nice gal" incumbent who is doing a good job keeping in touch with constituents.

It may be tough to rev up your own righteous anger against a hard-working first-time candidate whose positions are basically the same as yours. You may find yourself asking, "Why am I putting in so much work to defeat someone who'd do an okay job?" You can't win if you trap yourself into this self-defeating line of reasoning. Concentrate on your differences. Focus on the positive points in your own campaign. Seeking a job promotion in the "real world" often involves the same kind of situation; you compete against someone you know and admire. Positive thoughts about an opponent must not hold you back from throwing yourself wholeheartedly into the competition.

You may find it hard to excite people about your race if you and your opponent share the same basic support bases. They may pass over your campaign for a more interesting one if both you and your opponent are "right on the issues" and either of you would do a credible job. If no woman has previously held the position you seek, that should stir some feminist support to your banner, but it won't persuade many voters by itself.*

---

* Campaigns in which female candidates face male candidates strong on women's issues are troublesome choices and controversial within women's groups. Republican Congresswoman Nancy Johnson of Connecticut, a pro-choice six-year state senator from a Democratic district defeated a liberal Democrat in a 1982 race for Congress despite lack of support from women and women's organizations. According to *Women as Candidates in American Politics*, the WCF backed Johnson only in the primary, NWPC endorsed neither candidate, and NOW endorsed Johnson's opponent. With support from the Republican party and business community, Johnson outspent him and won the election.

In-depth polling is crucial for developing a winning strategy for this kind of race. Identify areas in which your opponent is vulnerable. Develop your strengths. Find out through polling who and where the undecided voters are and hone in on them through targeted mailings, phoning, ads and door-to-door canvassing. Smile a lot. Shake a lot of hands.

79

Avoid falling for the "ladies first" ploy; it is not to your advantage on the speaker's platform. Don't be tricked by well-intended or pretended gallantry on the part of your opponent.

If you follow your opponent to the lectern, you can refute arguments raised and have the last word. Insist on an equal opportunity to speak last.

Another "ladies first":

I asked a Burmese why women, after centuries of following their men, now walk ahead. He said there were many unexploded land mines since the war. — Robert Mueller

80

Don't be discouraged by what you hear or read in the newspapers about how well your opponent is doing; it's often wishful thinking or creative advertising. Politics is a game in which candidates try to fake out their opponents and their supporters. You are a player and need to put up a good front. But candidates who inflate their balloons too full of hot air end up losing credibility.

A couple of months before the November 1990 election, Steve Duin of the *Oregonian* gave gubernatorial candidate Barbara Roberts' campaign this advice, "Dial 234-7491. That's right: Dial-A-Prayer. Because right now, Babs doesn't have a prayer of winning this race." Five days later, he called her "a lightweight" who had run a "miserable campaign," using the adjectives "outclassed, inept and inexperienced."

The new governor's triumphant victory speech on election night was enlivened by a quote from Duin's column. Duin wrote a marvelous mea culpa column a short time later, saying he had placed too much value on the "power of the purse" and not enough on Roberts' charisma, her ability to "romance a crowd," to work them like a rock star, recalling adjectives he had used early in her race of "vibrant, visceral, visible."

Fear, paranoia, and jumping-to-hasty-conclusions are perennial campaign tendencies. Every candidate gets spooked, often on rumors planted by opposing forces. Like small animals who make their hair stand on end to appear larger and more threatening to their enemies, campaigns exaggerate their strengths to psych out the opposition.

As Yogi Berra said, "It ain't over 'till it's over."

81

Refute an opponent's charge publicly if people will assume you are acquiescing to the merits of the issue without response. You can give an accusation more attention and dignity than it deserves by discussing it. However, if allegations are made on prime-time TV or in newspaper headlines, you must respond immediately and reflectively or your credibility will slide.

During recent election years, negative campaigning has become the number one topic in campaign circles. The Willy Horton ads used in the 1988 Bush-Dukakis race have become a benchmark by which other negative campaigning is measured. Symbols and values are the principle target in most negative ads.

Women are advised that negative tactics backlash faster for them than for men (as in "emotional," "shrill," and "bitchy" stereotypes). Discussion regarding applicable election laws and when and if to initiate negative campaigning against your opponent is contained at tip 76. This tip addresses responses to negative tactics used against you.

Most of the dialogue about negative campaigning is centered on *major* races. These accusations and insinuations play in television or radio ads heard by vast audiences. To these you must respond. Then do something positive. If you can, poll to see if the accusations are cutting into your base or sliding off. Don't allow yourself to be kept on the defensive; find a way to change the subject. Don't be afraid to admit a mistake and move forward. Making lame excuses never sits well with the public.

A different problem confronts the candidate in a lower-visibility campaign in which criticisms or accusations are made in a private letter or to a small audience. The rebuttal to this type of accusation could get more publicity than the original statement and you'd be giving your opponent exposure. Consult your advisors on this. Stick to the facts when you make responses, keep them short and sweet. The appearance of "the lady doth protest too much, methinks" (*Hamlet*, Shakespeare) can result if not handled carefully.

Texas Governor Ann Richards refused to answer campaign charges made against her that she had used drugs as well as alcohol. (She spoke openly of her prior addiction to alcohol.) Even though Richards won, many observers felt that these unanswered charges hurt her. Her media consultant said, "It was more credible for a woman to take the high road, to say she was refusing to discuss this matter out of conscience."

Republican nominee Linda Chavez of Maryland aimed what the media characterized as "one of the dirtiest campaigns of 1986" against Democratic nominee Barbara Mikulski, but never made significant gains by doing so. Chavez "kicked off her campaign emphasizing her own traditional status as a mother of three sons and describing Mikulski as a 'San Francisco-style feminist,' then went on to make a major campaign issue out of an episode in 1981 when Mikulski had hired an Australian radical feminist as an aide in her congressional office," says *Momentum: Women in American Politics Now*. "It appeared to some observers that what Chavez was questioning was not so much Mikulski's judgment as her sexuality, but when reporters questioned Chavez, she said no such inference was intended." Mikulski, who had already served in the U.S. House of Representatives for 10 years, and prior to that, many years on the Baltimore City Council, and was already well-known to most of her voters and won handily.

The male opponent of first-time candidate Allyson Schwartz in Pennsylvania's 4th State Senate District in 1990 circulated only to white neighborhoods a photograph* of Allyson darkened to make her look black, which she isn't. Her black supporters were outraged. On a flyer containing pictures of American flags, white crosses and Betsy Ross, Schwartz's opponent said, "Philadelphia. Birthplace of the American Flag . . . Allyson Schwartz doesn't share our values. And doesn't deserve to be our Senator." In smaller type: "It's true. Schwartz would permit our flag to be burned so that a few radicals could abuse the rights that thousands have died to protect."

---

* Watch out for unflattering photographs—stringy or mussed-up hair is common for women. Use hair spray before campaign appearances or get a new permanent. An unfriendly editor used a photo of Wilsonville (Oregon) City Council candidate Friedgard Van Eck showing her hair at its most unkempt (which may or may not have been a purposeful choice on the editor's part); she won anyway, with a $2,000 budget, gaining the most votes in a field of eight by her door-to-door campaigning and strong stand on a controversial urban renewal issue.

After six weeks of negative attacks, Schwartz responded by calling her opponent's tactics "anti-Semitic." Then she was publicly admonished by some conservative Jewish groups that she was overreacting, going too far. Even though she never retaliated "in a sustained way," as a *Philadelphia Inquirer* reporter put it, Allyson Schwartz continued her dynamic personal campaigning. Based on impressive credentials which brought her the endorsement of the *Inquirer* and many others, she won one of the most closely watched and expensive contests in the state by a 3-2 margin. Even before she was sworn in to office, political insiders were taking bets on her political future.*

The distinction between misrepresentation of your record and truthful use of your record must be made. It's a legitimate campaign practice to portray your record in its most unflattering light; you will need to have a ready explanation of your stands or actions. Be sure you have researched your own record so you are not taken by surprise.

Be prepared with offensive and defensive strategies and responses *before* your opponent's camp strikes with negative campaigning, and jump into action before irreparable damage is done to your campaign. Surprise is the element which most throws a candidate off-stride. Have an ace in the hole as a means to switch the focus of attention onto something else more positive. Try humor.

---

* Nationally-syndicated columnist Ellen Goodman of the *Boston Globe* profiled Allyson Schwartz in a column published three weeks before the election as a prototype of a new wave of women candidates motivated to run against anti-abortion incumbents. *Philadelphia Daily News* columnist Jill Porter said this: "Schwartz, 42, the mother of two sons and a social worker by training, is symbolic of this political season and a harbinger of the future. She's the best of the new genre of candidates: female, rooted in the women's movement, motivated by a commitment to issues rather than a promotion of self. She admits to harboring political ambitions all of her life..."

TIPS 82 - 85
Media

82

Have your scheduler contact every editor who will make endorsements in your race immediately after filing deadline to schedule an endorsement interview. Determine the special demands and interests of each newspaper; all are different. Many newspapers will carry on their endorsement process without you if you don't seek them out.

People believe what they see in print. Newspaper endorsements help sway from 2% to 7% of readers, according to national research. In a tight race, this could make the difference between a win or loss.

Endorsements have the most impact in low-profile races with little-known candidates. (Also when they defy conventional wisdom, such as a Democratic newspaper making a surprise endorsement of a Republican.) If you can persuade a friendly newspaper to make an early endorsement, the prestige can help your credibility. Time the printing of your flyers for the last couple of weeks of canvassing to make use of such endorsements, if possible. In large districts, schedule interviews by geographical district to save travel time.

One of the things a statewide candidate notices immediately is the dearth of female editors at daily newspapers. Journalism is still a male-dominated field.

Every newspaper conducts its endorsement process differently. Editors usually ask their political reporters for input and opinions. Some combine endorsement interviews with a photo session and a news interview, but most newspapers keep those processes entirely separate. Some editors may talk to you more than once. Sometimes a single editor does the candidate endorsement interview, other newspapers will have two or three or even 10 editors in the room with you.

In addition to a standard press kit of background information about your campaign and your issues, some editors want to see your budget and a list of your major contributors and supporters. Some will ask you for the dirt on your opponent (who will undoubtedly be given the same opportunity.) Editors will want to know why you're running and why they should endorse you instead of your opposition. Some do follow-up reference calls.

Find out the protocol in your local community. If it's fair game—and it usually is—to have pillars of the community call newspaper editors *whom they know* to lobby on your behalf, by all means have them do so.

83

Seek unusual ways to get air time and press coverage. Free publicity is especially important for candidates on stringent budgets. Release your weekly schedule to the press, radio and TV stations, hold press conferences on developing issues, think up different angles that will grab human interest coverage. Don't be shy about using your family; the public loves evidence of a happy home.

Save press conferences for hard breaking news; once bitten by a candidate who cries wolf the reporters won't be fooled again. Be friendly and open; don't ever lie. But don't just wait for a reporter to call you: Pick up the phone now and then to call one of your press contacts, ask what's going on and pass along a bit of gossip.

Think of ways to give reporters and columnists a new angle, a story that could appear in the feature section, the sports section, something for the business news, a travel story. Do you have a recipe that may be pertinent or newsworthy? Call the cooking editor. Is your business doing something that readers would find interesting? Call the business reporter. How about your family? Find the hook. Brainstorm with your media director.

Editors always need fillers for specific segments or pages. A daily paper, for example, might have a page devoted to gardening on Mondays, on interior design Tuesdays. On Wednesdays, health and fitness. The editor *needs* copy to fill those spaces every week. Holidays also represent very specific needs. Try to think of an unusual story idea and you'll have the potential to reach a broader audience than the news and editorial pages.

For TV, think of story ideas for their *visual* potential. Would it make good pictures? When interviewed on radio or TV for informal talk-show programs, carry along a biographical sketch and a list of possible questions the interviewer might ask you. If your host is not prepared, this may help raise the points you want to discuss. When being interviewed on TV, look at the reporter, not the camera.

Remember, 75% to 80% of all news is planted. Be persistent. Publicity will come.

"There is only one thing in the world worse than being talked about, and that is not to be talked about," said Oscar Wilde.

84

Keep yourself informed of media coverage in your race, both news and editorial, everywhere in your district. **Contract with a newspaper clipping service. Also a TV and radio service, or find housebound volunteers to monitor TV and radio coverage.**

A staff member or regular volunteer will need to screen the maze of newspaper clippings and television/radio reports coming to the campaign office and bring significant items to your attention daily. Set your wake-up radio for the news and skim the paper before you leave home every morning to avoid being caught unprepared on relevant issues.

Also inform yourself about the reporters covering your race. You should know more about the reporters than they do about you. Where do they live? What issues are important in their area? Do they have young children? If they've won special recognition, what for? What prejudices and hidden agendas do they bring to their craft? Find common grounds and make your relationships personal. Countless voters will form their judgments of you by the way the media presents you to them.

Good personal relationships are invaluable. Getting to know the reporters should be one of the most enjoyable parts of your campaign. They are always interesting people.

85

Decide in advance exactly where you want to be when the earliest election returns are broadcast. **Reporters love to capture candidates' reactions to election results. Have alternative phrases prepared for up or down trends or else find a private place to sequester yourself during the early evening hours.**

Have both a short victory speech and a concession speech planned. Write these speeches down, or at least key words, on different colored cue cards that you can put in your purse or tuck inside your bra. The words you're looking for may not spill forth automatically when the time comes. Even if you'd rather not make a speech, your supporters need you to. Introduce your family and campaign manager. Consider renting a portable mike; it gives you something to hold onto and carries your words with authority.

Traditional election night protocol calls for the candidate, her family, close friends and advisors to wait in a secluded suite close to her victory party. When returns establish a trend, the candidate makes an appearance. She's besieged by media, who have kept their respectful distance earlier while she relaxed in privacy. Unless you're running for governor or congress, though, if you have been engaged in a hotly-contested battle you'll probably want to spend most of the evening at your own party visiting with friends and supporters who turn out to wish you well.

If you lose the race, you'll need to make a concession /congratulations telephone call to your opponent. (Be sure someone locates that phone number ahead of time, along with phone numbers for key places to call for late-breaking ballot counts.)

"Waiting for election returns is like a hen sitting on a nest—except that the hen uses better judgment than a politician," says actor Charles Coburn in the 1944 movie *Wilson.* "She never cackles until after she's laid an egg."

TIPS 86 - 94

Candidate Personal Matters

86

Expect severe disruption of your family life. If you are a mother without full-time help at home, you will need to prepare your family for significant changes when you hit the campaign trail. It's crucial that your spouse be sympathetic to your political aspirations.

Your personal life takes a back seat during a contested campaign. Everyone in your close circle of family and friend will be affected. In some ways, it is easier for a single woman (divorced, widowed, never married) to campaign than for a married one.

If you are seeking a full-time elective position, both the campaign itself and holding office will change your life. The biggest effect of the campaign, for most households, will be that for three, six, nine months, you may often be absent from home during or shortly after the dinner hour. You may need to attend more night meetings and early breakfasts than ever before. If you do a door-to-door campaign, every weekday and weekend afternoon will be taken as well.

"Most Americans have long ago resolved the tensions between feminism and family," says E.J. Dionne Jr. in *Why Americans Hate Politics*. "They're for both. Polls make clear that by overwhelming margins, Americans believe that women are in the work force to stay and this, on balance, is a good thing. The same polls also show that Americans worry that economic pressures are forcing both parents out of the home too much. Americans don't want a debate on the respective glories of 'the traditional family' and feminism; they want to build a world where men and women are treated equally and where kids get treated well, too."

You should do five things to prepare for a campaign:

1) Discuss your goals and motivation with your husband to be sure he understands and supports your candidacy.
2) Talk to a previous candidate for the office you seek to determine what the time demands are for your kind of race.
3) Make plans for needed shifts in household routines with everyone involved before you announce for office.
4) Include your family in your campaign schedule. Make time for them.
5) Use patience, understanding and humor in preparing your responses to questions (which *will* come) as to how your family's needs are being taken care of, especially if you have young children.

Questions will most likely come from an older woman or one of your own age who will be saying to herself, "I couldn't possibly do/have done this. My kids need(ed) me at home." Be sure she understands how important your family is to you, too, and that you plan to honor traditional family holidays. She's probably envious of your freedom, and it also means she cares.

When Pat Schroeder was first elected to Congress her youngest child was two, and she was besieged by questions about her family's care. Schroeder was surprised when one of the first things Congresswoman Bella Abzug said to her was, "I hear you have two little kids." When Schroeder said yes, Abzug asked, "How are you going to do it?"

87

Anticipate enormous curiosity about your relationship with your spouse or partner. Develop ready answers to "What does your husband think about your running?" and "Who's taking care of the house?" If you're not married, questions may be less direct but the interest is no less intense.

Your friends and enemies will wonder, whether or not they ask you directly: Who's cooking the meals? Cleaning house? How does your husband like being Mr. Sally Brown? You may ask yourself some of these same questions. Being the spouse of a candidate of either sex is not easy, but it's a new role for husbands and there are no established traditions to follow.

Anthony Morella, attorney in private practice and husband of Republican Representative Connie Morella of Maryland, "is a former congressional aide who ran other successful election campaigns before he helped launch his wife's race," said a recent *Common Cause* magazine article. "So he can afford to be big about it if he gets invitations from the Congressional Club on pink stationery. Do important Washingtonians treat him like part of the woodwork? *Au contraire*, he says,—half the time they assume he's the one in Congress. Or they make a big fuss over him because male congressional spouses are so rare."

The husbands of Madeline Kunin of Vermont and Kay Orr of Nebraska, the only two spouses of women governors in 1988, were interviewed by the magazine *New Choices for the Best Years*. The "Two First Gentlemen" article speaks of the innumerable receptions and ceremonies Arthur Kunin and Bill Orr attended, standing at the sides of their wives, shaking hands and smiling, and the need for them to pay the bills, learn to cook and maintain their households.

Society is still used to having the man speak for the woman, Arthur Kunin was quoted as saying. "The point I want to make is that she is the governor; she is the important one." Taking that kind of back-seat role may be difficult for many husbands to accept, and just as hard for their wives to assume for themselves.

Unmarried women candidates have it easier in some ways, harder in others. They usually don't have to worry about family, but they may have to deal with morbid curiosity about their sex life or lack thereof. The most insidious aspects are speculations about sexual preference.

Lesbian women are fearful that their constituencies will vote against them if their sexual preference becomes known, and in parts of the country, homophobia runs high. The issue of homosexuality itself has only recently been publicly discussed, so it is to be expected that many hostile feelings will surface when sexual orientation becomes an issue in a campaign.

In Maine, two open lesbians ran for the state senate in 1990. "Dale McCormick and Sive Nielan challenged incumbents in campaigns that turned very nasty and in which lesbian-baiting was prevalent," said the *Now National Times*. While Nielan was unsuccessful, McCormick was elected in a district "very rural and considered very conservative." In a letter to the editor of the local paper, the incumbent's brother called McCormick an "insult to womanhood and motherhood" because she was a lesbian and had not experienced the pain of childbirth.

The tactic backfired. "Mothers from around the district wrote to the paper expressing their outrage...and support for McCormick," the *NOW Times* said. The lesson of her campaign, McCormick said, was, "If I can do it, anybody can do it. I've wanted to be in elected office since I was quite young, but felt that option was closed off to me because of my gender and sexual orientation. I began to work through the mental barriers. What finally pushed me over the last barrier was the *Webster* decision.* To quote Shirley Chisholm, 'We women must put aside our petty reluctances and run for office.'"

---

* *Webster vs. Reproductive Health Services*, a Missouri case decided by the U.S. Supreme Court in July 1989, expanded states' authority to regulate and restrict access to abortions. A May 1991 Supreme Court opinion, *Rust vs. Sullivan*, prohibits abortion-related counseling, referrals or advocacy by clinics which receive federal funds.

Candidates or potential candidates who are lesbian should seek counsel from a local gay or lesbian group and/or from a paid consultant on how to determine what reaction they might expect on the issue of sexual orientation from voters in their district. Chances are, if you already are an elected official before the voters learn of your sexual orientation it will make little difference to most of them. To some it will make a great difference.

For first time candidates who are lesbian and do not yet have a visible public record, the issue should be handled carefully. It is the same basic challenge facing all first-time candidates: you start with a blank page and the voters color it in as they learn things about you. Your chances for election are best if the first lines drawn on that blank page represent stability and traditional values, attributes which you have *in common* with most voters, rather than those on which you differ. (Touch hope and pride buttons; avoid anger and fear.)

88

Reach an up-front understanding of what involvement your family will commit to the campaign to save tempers and staff misunderstandings later. **While spouses of female candidates are not expected to play the same role as spouses of males traditionally have, campaigns always need whatever help they can get and are pushy by nature. Protect and include your family by getting advance agreement on ground rules with all concerned.**

Enlist children, cousins, nieces, nephews, aunts, uncles, parents, in-laws of every age. Get them out meeting voters, shaking hands and talking about your race. Have them carry banners, hand out leaflets, lick stamps, make phone calls, knock on doors, be the guests of honor at neighborhood coffees. Voters like this; teenagers and grandparents have a special appeal. A letter addressed to older women in your district from your mother, or one from your father to the older men, can be especially effective.

Voters will be pleased that your family is supportive and working for your election. A family member—no matter how distant—represents you personally. Be sure each relative carries a supply of flyers with your name and office printed prominently to hand out to everyone they meet. Some will also want to carry pledge envelopes.

Find a specific role in the campaign for every willing and able adult family member. That role might be sponsoring a special fund-raising event, heading up a post-card writing campaign or securing lawn sign locations in the west half of your county. If you don't locate a niche for them, they will soon be knocking heads with campaign staff and other volunteers in the search for a way to help. Whatever the role is, the assignment should be specific and reduced to writing, almost like a job description.

Your family and staff will both be happier if you keep your family out of campaign strategy and management. Campaign managers and consultants frequently complain about meddling family members, especially spouses and precocious college-age children. Some attribute this perennial conflict between staff and families to the easy access to the candidates that families have, and their picking up mumbling and grumbling from supporters and friends who are always second-guessing what's going on in a campaign. Families may also feel jealous of the time the campaign is demanding.

So keep your family focused on the jobs they've been assigned. Have them help you with your fund raising and meeting voters when appropriate.

On the other hand, you will probably rely on your family's help for nearly every aspect of the race in a small campaign. Some campaigns are run completely from home as joint family ventures.

89

Find a part-time housekeeper before the campaign crunch hits. Women candidates have difficulty shaking guilt feelings for not doing their share of household duties; such tendencies must be overcome for the duration of the campaign. Finding household help early will allow training and a shakedown period before the heaviest campaign demands begin.

A female candidate who has small children at home might seriously consider employing a cook and general household helper or having a relative join the household temporarily. Even when help is secured, it is usually the woman of the house who smooths out difficulties and seeks solutions when employees are unexpectedly absent.

If you don't have children, you should find outside assistance with cleaning unless your husband agrees to assume that duty. If you're single, find help for at least four or five hours a month. You can't do everything, and it will give you a lift to walk into a clean house when you get home.

Don't think that those who get elected to Congress have escaped traditional household tasks entirely. Congresswoman Nita Lowey's juggling of schedules made the newspaper when Congress recessed on a Friday for Jewish holidays. Rep. Lowey caught a 1 p.m. shuttle from Washington bound for her home in Westchester County, New York, but the plane was delayed. "The holiday begins at sundown Friday night," she told a newspaper reporter. "I didn't get home until 3:30. I ran out to the market and put together a quick dinner so I could be in synagogue by 6 p.m." Her mother-in-law brought part of the dinner, Lowey said.

For Congresswoman Olympia Snowe of Maine, cooking is not a problem. Since marrying Governor "Jock" McKernan in February 1989, Snowe spends Tuesday through Thursday nights in Washington when Congress is in session and the rest of the time she and McKernan, a former Congressman, live in four rooms on the second floor of the governor's mansion. The Governor's regular week-day cook often "leaves reheatable meals for the weekends," *Down East* magazine says. "When they do fix their own food, McKernan cooks, Snowe cleans." They also call for Domino's Pizza delivery now and then.

90

Consider getting an unlisted home phone number and install an answering machine. To protect your privacy and screen out crank callers, either an answering device or an unlisted home phone, or both, may be needed.

Knowing who is on the line before you pick up the receiver gives you a few seconds to prepare your thoughts. Answering machines can also help you document what's been said. Keep in mind, however, that in becoming a candidate, you become a public person, and relinquish privacy in doing so.

An answering machine is also essential in every campaign office. You can't afford to miss a single call. If your campaign is being run primarily from your home, you may wish to install a separate campaign phone with a listed number and an answering machine. This will keep your family line free for family calls and make it easy to identify campaign phone expenses.

91

Upgrade your wardrobe and consider it a hidden, but unavoidable, personal campaign cost. **With thousands of eyes watching, you will want to look your best, which probably means buying some new clothes. Don't change your basic style; dress comfortably—especially your shoes (!)—and choose clothing that looks like you mean business.**

Be identifiable as a candidate without giving the impression, particularly if you're in a small local race, that you're putting on airs or think you're better than others. The women in your audience will notice what you wear and how your hair looks, whether the men do or not.

Wardrobe consultants have traditionally advised that "sweater" means secretary and "suit" means boss. Give yourself this test: Sit in a downtown restaurant and look out the window at people walking up and down the sidewalk. Guess what their occupations are. Which ones would you vote for? Borrow or rent a video camera and have a friend make a videotape of you walking down that same street, then watch the videotape in the privacy of your own home. Would you vote for yourself? Would your mother? Your father? (Assuming they didn't know you, of course.)

Take a friend whose taste you admire with you to shop for new clothes, and plan to spend $500 to $1,000. Before you go, study the styles of clothing worn by TV newswomen and female talk show hosts and the necklines and styles on photos of women elected officials. Set up an appointment with a fashion consultant or personal representative to help you find flattering color-coordinated outfits. Choose comfortable styles in perky colors. For television appearances, choose rough fabrics in deep blues, greens, reds and earth colors, avoiding whites and shiny materials.

In Geraldine Ferraro's book, *FERRARO My Story*, she speaks with humor and common sense about the problems her wardrobe posed. "I learned the slip lesson the hard way during a parade in New York...my dress had come up with my arms, leaving behind my slip...(a) television crew had focused its cameras on my hemline....'What is unusual about campaigning as a woman?' the loaded question came. And I was ready. 'Well, there are things that happen,' I said casually. 'For instance, if you're walking along in a parade and you raise you arm and your slip shows, people might be critical of you. No guy has a problem like that.'"

The only place Ferraro drew the line was against wearing slacks in public. She knew that could have offended people in conservative areas of the country. But she refused to be harnessed solely in suits or to stay away from short-sleeved dresses in the heat of summer. Her two rules were: "comfort and quiet good taste."

92

Get professional advice about your haircut and glasses early in the campaign. You'll be asking people to vote for you who will be seeing you for the first time. You have to be willing to conform to what society expects its public officials to look like. The first impression you make is the most important.

A trendy hair style, like a beard on a man, will trigger negative reactions from some voters. Most people don't want to see a high fashion model; they like flesh and blood human beings with personality and a few imperfections.* But voters carry an image in their minds of what they like to see; if you look too differently from the public's perceptions, you will lose votes.

The time to consider changes in a basic hair style, glasses or mode of dress is very early in the campaign, before you've had photos taken. Later you will need to stay with your basic image to avoid confusing the voters. Then you can ignore 99% of the advice you get about personal appearance with good conscience.

Have that early consultation be a complete make-over to see what it produces. Visit a beauty salon which matches your face with a variety of hair styles on a computer screen. Take along your favorite hairdresser and a style-conscious friend to help you choose. You will want a simple style you can reproduce yourself, maybe with a trim every three or four weeks and a new perm every three months.

Have at least one studio portrait taken which will be used over and over—in your press kit, on brochures, in voters' pamphlets, in speakers' programs, and on a poster blow-up for campaign office walls. You'll get sick of it. But like your basic stump speech, you'll need that photo to reinforce your image in voters' minds. Also have several good informal shots taken for use in brochures, newsletters and other publications.

---

* Stunning looks may be a hindrance to women on the campaign trail. An experiment with 125 college students as subjects concluded that "attractive women labor under an impediment in running for public office." Author Ann O'M. Bowman speculates in *Women and Politics* quarterly, Winter 1984, that perhaps the photos of female candidates jarred the stereotypical vision these young people had of what an elected official looks like. Good looks were still best for male candidates, however, based on the responses of these students.

93

Before you ever decided to run for office, you should have probed your own background and that of your family regarding past indiscretions that might come back to haunt you. You should develop a plan for handling adverse publicity which might be based on such charges. Opposition research is the fastest-growing segment of the political consulting industry. Since your opponent will probably research your background, you'd better do it yourself first.

For a hotly-contested race, find a reliable volunteer to look at your previous issue stands, business and organizational affiliations, letters written, income tax filings, periods of heavy drinking, business dealings. Extend this research to your spouse if married. Money will always be a sensitive issue in campaigns, so the source of your (and your husband's) money must be considered a potentially volatile issue.

Many female candidates have been skewered by public disclosure of their husband's finances: Nancy Kassebaum (who wasn't hurt badly because she and her husband were already separated); Geraldine Ferraro (who was put to the most bitter test of her vice-presidential candidacy by a howling, hungry press); Dianne Feinstein (who grew testy during her California gubernatorial race because reporters besieged her for disclosure about her husband's holdings and suggested he put them in a blind trust); and Eleanor Holmes Norton (whose husband hadn't filed federal income tax forms for several years, which was disclosed during her race for D.C. Congressional delegate.) Publicity about their husband's business dealings put all these candidates on the defensive and away from the focus of their campaigns.

The journalists' rule used to be that the private lives of elected officials were off the record unless directly related to their jobs. But that standard changed with Gary Hart's bid for the presidential nomination in 1984 when revelations about his personal life and a photo of his frolicking on a yacht off the coast of Florida made campaign history. Candidates beware: Indiscretions can be fatal.

94

Have a contingency plan for what you will do professionally if you lose the election, even if you don't tell another soul about it. Don't expect to lose, but in the off-chance you do, the plunge will be softened if you have a fall-back plan. This is a must for peace of mind.

"Show me a good loser and I'll show you a loser," is another political axiom. That doesn't mean you should be a totally unprepared. Expect postpartum depression—win or lose. Also plan to get away from the telephone for a few days after the election so you can completely unwind.

If you don't win, remember that 60 percent of the people in Congress lost a major race at one time. Be sure you gather yourself together enough to convene a critique session to identify what went wrong and right for your campaign. Consider hiring a pollster to conduct a focus group or follow-up poll to ask why people voted as they did in your race. But don't wait too long—voters' memories can be very short.

A loss is not the end of the world, but it's no fun. You will need a new goal to work toward. The best time to think clearly, to come up with innovative ideas as to what that might be, is before you're feeling numb with defeat.

But of course you are going to win.

TIPS 95 - 101
Everything Else

95

Know you will be criticized—it is an unavoidable and unending rite of passage to seeking and serving in public office. **Sooner or later, unless you go into hibernation, you will be criticized in private, in public, in print, and on the airwaves.**

Don't let criticism throw you or divert you from your mission. Remember that you are in the public eye for a purpose. With experience, you will learn to build a protective shell, to grow more thick-skinned. You must learn not to take the criticism personally. It will be your actions which are faulted, not you as a person. If you are extra thin-skinned, stay out of elective politics.

"Women tend to be more devastated and taken aback by criticism than men are," a first-time candidate said. "Men seem to be raised to deal with criticism as not personal. We women tend to be more surprised when misrepresentation and lies are used against us."

Miss Truman is a unique American phenomenon with a pleasant voice of little size and fair quality... — Music Critic Paul Hume

I have read your lousy review of Margaret's concert...Some day I hope to meet you. When that happens you'll need a new nose, a lot of beefsteak for black eyes, and perhaps a supporter below.

— Harry S Truman

96

Expect some erosion and defection from your support base, occasionally by individuals you counted on as friends. **"Politics makes strange bedfellows," is a truism which newcomers find hard to accept when its ramifications hit home. Your opponent will be getting some surprises, too, by people he or she knows who end up supporting you.**

The disappointment you need to brace yourself for the strongest is for a woman you expected to back you to come out for your opponent. You will feel hurt, angry, betrayed and shattered. You will want to tell her how you feel, but this is exactly what you must not do. There is no way you can know what pressures, former friendships, neighborhood ties, or even promises of glory were brought to bear on her. Do not take it personally. Now she owes you one.

"The hardest thing to learn in life is which bridge to cross and which to burn," said David Russell. Grit your teeth, swallow your pride, and don't let this woman or anyone else except your closest advisors know how deeply this hurts. Welcome to the hard realities of politics. If you handle yourself with dignity, you may find her support behind you next time. Whatever you do, don't burn this bridge and make an enemy for life over it. On your side of the ledger, surprises will come from people you never thought would support you.

Allegiances and power deals and people calling in their chits—situations over which you have no control—are bound to cause defections in a hotly-contested race. Remember that the world doesn't revolve around your contest, so try to put it in perspective.

Some of the tough decisions you have to make may also lose you support. Dealing with controversial issues during a campaign can be good preparation for serving in office. You learn what things you really care about and to ignore less important things.

97

Learn to take the peaks and valleys in stride; campaigns are teeter-totters with abrupt ups and downs. Sometimes you'll feel more devastated than you've ever felt in your life, but other times you'll be sitting on top of the world.

The ups and downs of a campaign can hit first-time candidates like a battering ram. It's also a special shock to have your personal defeats and triumphs shared with hundreds or even thousands of people through the media.

Events which are most apt to trigger your emotions include the entry or withdrawal of opponents in your race, newspaper reports of how much money you've raised in comparison to your opponent, the size of the crowd at your fund-raising event, polling results, favorable or unfavorable publicity for either you or your opponent, endorsing of your opponent by someone you thought was supporting you, endorsements by prominent individuals, organizations or newspapers for either you or your opponent.

Try to find a goal you can meet without regard to the whims of the voters; for example, to run a strong, credible campaign with a manageable deficit. Remind yourself why you are running and of the valuable contribution you are making to your community and the democratic process by making this race.

When the race doesn't appear to be going well, everyone you meet will have advice. Smile and thank them and move on to the next voter.

When things look good, both you and your staff may have a tendency to slack off a little, to feel over-confident. Don't. Until the last ballot is counted, nobody knows what the voters will decide.

Ask yourself: Am I doing the best I can? If the answer is yes, then concentrate on carrying through with your part of the bargain with head held high.

98

Keep going: Persevere, one step at a time, each day at a time, doing what you can, even when the odds don't look promising. **Unlike other challenges you face in your life, this one has a clear beginning and end—and sometimes a surprise finish. Do what you have to do. Stick with it.**

Even if the earth is buckling beneath you, keep going, slowly and steadily, facing forward. Never look back.

"I studied the lives of great men and famous women," Harry Truman said, "and I found that the men and women who got to the top were those who did the jobs they had in hand, with everything they had of energy and enthusiasm and hard work." You wouldn't have gotten this far without quantities of energy and enthusiasm and hard work. Now all you need to do is see the contest through.

Stay with your original campaign plan. If a consultant advises a change based on new information, that becomes your new plan and you stick with that. But don't panic and try to run three or four campaigns. It doesn't work. Don't let unexpected events throw you. Patience and fortitude in raising money, meeting voters, and knowing your issues will count in the long haul. Leave the strategy decisions to the people you've hired to make them.

"That which you choose to do, do well," advises *Political Campaigning: A New Decade*, the NWPC campaign manual. "No one thing you do will insure you win, just as no one thing you do will mean you lose." It is the composite whole which makes the difference—the hundreds of hands you've shaken, the umpteen times your name has been mentioned on the radio, the countless unknown voters who review your literature and say to their friends, "I'm going to vote for her. She looks honest to me."

Remember: It was the tortoise who won the race, not the hare.

99

> *View yourself as a lightbulb everyone else needs to touch for energy and recharging.* This will get enormously tiring for you. For the duration of the campaign, you'll need to stay "on stage" everywhere you go, even the grocery store. Regardless of how many excellent people work for you, the campaign personality, dynamics, and tone will be decided by the pace and aura you set.

Home will be the one place you can climb down from the platform, kick off your shoes and put on your blue jeans. You need somewhere to unwind and home will usually be that place. That's why, in a major race, it's important to keep your family life separate from the campaign.

Don't try to be supermom. Recognize that every lightbulb burns out if not recharged. Find a way to meet your own energy and emotional needs. Close the doors to your bedroom, unhook the phone, and sleep around the clock. Take a long hike out of doors if you can spare the time—vigorous physical exercise can clear your mind miraculously. Try watching a tear-jerker movie and cry your heart out, or find an old-time comedy guaranteed to make you laugh. Being around preschoolers, pre-adolescents or college age young people can be invigorating just to listen to them talk.

But it's your show going on out there, and it can't play without you. You have the lead role. The other actors and actresses are awaiting their cues from you, and if you're off your stride or out of circulation for long, they may be too.

Your campaign staff and key volunteers need your strokes and spoken words of appreciation, your words of cheer. They don't see the same global picture of the campaign that you do, they don't have audiences clapping and supporters admonishing them to "Go give 'em hell!" Even when you feel totally drained, you've got to find the energy to put up a good front and give your staff encouragement.

"How come all the parties are for Jewel?" five-year-old Laura asked her mother when they drove me to yet another wine and cheese fund-raising event during one of my campaigns. It gave me a new perspective.

Here were all these people hosting festivities for me day after day, and I had been starting to think of it as work!

As your campaign nears the finish line, more and more of your time will be spent personally reaching out to voters. If you're employed on a regular job, take vacation time or leave without pay for the final two or three weeks. Spend every possible moment shaking hands and handing out flyers with your name, office, and photo prominently displayed. Include late endorsements in this brochure if possible. Get all the media coverage you can.

Listen to the voters. Look them in the eye. Give them a friendly smile. The strongest vote motivator is personal contact with the candidate. Each person you talk to will have half a dozen friends or uncles and cousins who vote. Your personal warmth will go a long way toward drawing hands toward the tiny box behind your name on the ballot.

100

Get out of politics if running for office ceases to be fun. Like any other job, campaigning won't be enjoyable all the time. But if you find you don't like being around people constantly, or you aren't entertained by the politics-as-theater in which you play a part, choose another calling. On the other hand, if you're undeterred by the preceding cautions, GO FOR IT. You are needed!

Politics is:

LEADERSHIP	FICKLE	WAR
POWER	THEATER	OPPORTUNITY
HARD	COMPETITIVE SPORT	NOT ALWAYS FAIR
	CIVIC DUTY	

It's not for everyone. Another political maxim: "Politics is dependent on a never-ending supply of people who don't know what they're in for."

"Some people won't get burned out in 30 years, some people get burned out in three," Carol Bellamy told the authors of *Momentum: American Women in Politics NOW*. "One of the reasons I left the (state) senate and ran for the presidency of the (New York City) Council was I thought to myself that too many of the debates each year were sounding like the debates of the previous year, and maybe I was losing some of the passion I thought you needed to have—that doesn't mean you have to be screaming, it just means you have to have some passion, you have to feel...you need to get up in the morning and say, 'Boy, I'm going to—in my own stupid way—save the world today.'"

101

Invite everyone to attend your election night celebration. Make election night your finest hour, regardless of what has happened during the race. This is the time to thank people for the thousands of hours and dollars and prayers they have offered on your behalf.

Try to find a way to acknowledge and thank everyone who assisted your campaign in any way. An amazing number of folks care deeply about your winning because they believe you will make an outstanding public official. They will appreciate being asked to your party, even if they choose to watch the returns from the comfort of their own homes.

And after it's all over, search for other ways to remember those supporters. Holiday cards with pictures of you and your family in an informal, personal pose will be treasured. Congresswoman Pat Schroeder of Colorado sends out cards each year with pictures of her husband, son, daughter, dog and herself that undoubtedly hang proudly from countless mirrors and refrigerator doors.

Everyone who has been a member of your team deserves special treatment election night. An idea: Have laminated name tags made up with your campaign logo, the person's name and what he or she did on the campaign. A volunteer with a graphics-capable computer could print these ready for laminating.

Find an hour or two to spend alone with staff and key volunteers in the 24 hours before the polls close. It might be pizza at the office on election eve, an early evening buffet at someone's home or an hour together at the office on election day while a volunteer answers the phones.

Take time out to reflect, with those who've worked closest to you, where you started and how far you've come. No matter what the election results, how you conducted the campaign will matter—the battles fought, the laughter shared, the lessons learned.

You have traveled a long road together. It is a journey you will remember for a lifetime.

Politics is a challenging sport. Have fun with it. Now, get out there and win!

BIBLIOGRAPHY

Barber, James David, *The Presidential Character, Predicting Performance in the White House*, Prentice Hall, ©1972

Bullitt, Stimson, *To Be A Politician*, Yale University Press, ©1977

Carroll, Susan J., *Women as Candidates in American Politics,* Indiana University Press, ©1985

Carroll, Susan J. and Strimling, Wendy S., *Women's Routes to Elective Office, A Comparison with Men's*, Eagleton Institute of Politics, Rutgers University, 1981

Carter, Jimmy, *Why Not the Best?*, Broadman Press, ©1975

Carter, Rosalynn, *First Lady from Plains*, Houghton Mifflin Company, ©1984

Conway, Jill K., Bourque, Susan C., Scott, Joan W., *Learning About Women, Gender, Politics, & Power*, University of Michigan Press, ©1987

Covey, Stephen R., *The 7 Habits of Highly Effective People*, Simon & Schuster Inc, ©1989

Cuomo, Mario M., *Diaries of Mario M. Cuomo, The Campaign for Governor*, Random House, ©1984

Dionne, E.J. Jr., *Why Americans Hate Politics*, Simon & Schuster, ©1991

Ferraro, Geraldine, with Linda Bird Francke, *Ferraro, My Story*, Bantam Books, ©1985

Fowler, Linda L.and McClure, Robert, *Political Ambition: Who Decides To Run for Congress?*, New Haven: Yale University Press, ©1989

Hartman, Susan M., *From Margin to Mainstream: American Women and Politics Since 1960*, Alfred A. Knopf, Inc., ©1989

Heilbrun, Carolyn G., *Writing a Woman's Life*, Ballatine Books, ©1988

Hennig, Margaret and Jardim, Anne, *The Managerial Woman*, Doubleday, ©1977

Higgins, George V., *Victories*, Henry Holt and Co, Inc., ©1990

Lash, Joseph P., *Eleanor and Franklin, The Story of Their Relationship Based on Eleanor Roosevelt's Private Papers,* W.W. Norton & Company, Inc., ©1971

LeVeness, Frank P., and Sweeney, Jane P., *Women Leaders in Contemporary U.S. Politics*, Lynne Rienner Publishers, Inc., Boulder, CO, ©1987

Kirkpatrick, Jeane J., *Political Woman*, Basic Books, Inc., ©1974

Koch, Edward I., *Mayor, An Autobiography*, Simon and Schuster, Inc., ©1984, 1985

Mandel, Ruth, *In the Running, The New Woman Candidate,* Ticknor & Fields, ©1981; Beacon Press paperback edition, 1983

Millett, Kate, *Sexual Politics*, Doubleday & Company, Inc., ©1970

National Directory of Women Elected Officials 1989, National Women's Political Caucus, ©1989

Noonan, Peggy, *What I Saw At The Revolution, A Political Life in the Reagan Era*, Ballatine Books, ©1990

Phillips, Michael, *The Seven Laws of Money*, Word Wheel and Random House, ©1974

Reinsch, J. Leonard, *Getting Elected: from Radio and Roosevelt to Television and Reagan*, Hippocrene Books, Inc., ©1988

Romney, Ronna & Harrison, Beppie, *Momentum: Women in American Politics NOW*, Crown Publishers, Inc., ©1988

Rossi, Alice S., *Feminists in Politics, A Panel Analysis of the First National Women's Conference*, Academic Press, Inc., ©1982

Stone, Irving, *They Also Ran, The Story of the Men Who Were Defeated for the Presidency*, Doubleday & Company, Inc., ©1966

Stuhler, Barbara, *NO REGRETS: Minnesota Women and the Joan Growe Senatorial Campaign*, Braemar Press, 32 E. Fillmore Ave, St. Paul, MN 55107, ©1986

Tannen, Deborah, *You Just Don't Understand, Women and Men in Conversation*, William Morrow and Company, Inc., ©1990

Whitney, Sharon, and Raynor, Tom, *Women in Politics*, Franklin Watts, ©1986

HOW-TO CAMPAIGN BOOKS

Allen, Cathy, *POLITICAL CAMPAIGNING: A New Decade*, (Campaign manual), ©1990, National Women's Political Caucus, 1275 K St., N.W. Suite 750, Washington, D.C. 20005; telephone (202) 898-1100

Beaudry, Ann, and Schaeffer, Bob, *Local and State Elections, The Guide to Organizing Your Campaign*, The Free Press, ©1986

Democratic National Committee, Campaign kit, 430 South Capitol, Washington, D.C. 20003, telephone (202) 863-8000

EMILY's List, *Thinking of Running for Congress? A Guide for Democratic Women*, ©1991, 1112 16th Street, N.W., Suite 750, Washington, D.C. 20036

Huseby, Sandy, *How to Win an Election, A Complete Guide to Running a Successful Campaign*, St. Martin's Press, ©1983

Kay, Beatrice, *Victory in the Voting Booth*, ETC Publications, ©1981

Lake, Celinda C., with Pat Callbeck Harper, *Public Opinion Polling, A Handbook for Public Interest and Citizen Advocacy Groups*, Island Press, ©1987

National Federation of Republican Women, *Campaign Manual*, 310 First Street S.E., Washington, D.C. 20003

National Federation of Republican Women, *Consider Yourself for Public Office*, ©1989, 310 First Street S.E., Washington, D.C. 20003; telephone (800) 424-9342

Paizis, Suzanne, *Getting Her Elected, A Political Woman's Handbook*, ©1977, Creative Editions Publishing Company, P.O.Box 22879, Sacramento, CA 95822

Palmer, H. J., *How to Run for Office*, Sandia Publishing Corp, Albuquerque, NM 87110, ©1989

Tevis, Nona Lake, *Only Winning Counts, A Practical Guide to Winning Elections in Your Community*, ©1988, R & M Publishing Company, 2235-C Fort Sedgwick, Petersburg, VA 23805

Trafton, Barbara M., *Women Winning, How to Run for Office*, The Harvard Common Press, Inc., ©1984

SOURCES OF "HOW-TO" MATERIALS

Democratic National Committee, 430 South Capitol, S.E., Washington, D.C. 20003; telephone (202) 863-8000

Fund for a Feminist Majority, 1600 Wilson Blvd, Suite 1102, Arlington, VA 22209; telephone (703) 522-2214; West Coast office, 8105 West Third, Los Angeles, CA 90048; telephone (213) 651-0495

National Organization for Women (NOW), 1000 16th Street, N.W., Suite 700, Washington, D.C. 20036; telephone (202) 331-0066

National Political Congress of Black Women, P.O. Box 411, Rancocus, NJ 08073; telephone (609) 871-1500

National Republican Coalition for Choice, 709 Second Street N.E., Suite 100, Washington, D.C. 20002; telephone (202) 543-0676

National Women's Political Caucus, 1275 K Street, N.W., Suite 750, Washington, D.C. 20005; telephone (202) 898-1100

Republican National Committee, 310 First Street, S.E., Washington, D.C. 20003; telephone (202) 863-8500

Toastmasters International, Inc., 23182 Arroyo Vista, Rancho Margarita, CA 92688; telephone (714) 858-8255

Women's Campaign Fund, 1601 Connecticut Avenue N.W., Suite 800, Washington, D.C. 20009; telephone (202) 234-3700

MISCELLANEOUS CAMPAIGN AND ELECTION INFORMATION

American Association of Political Consultants, 5335 Wisconsin Avenue, N.W., Washington, D.C. 20015; telephone (202) 546-1564

Campaigns & Elections, a bi-monthly magazine, 1835 "K" Street, N.W., Suite 403, Washington, D.C. 20006; telephone (202) 331-3222

Campaign Magazine, 205 Pennsylvania Avenue, S.E., Washington, D.C. 20003; (202) 543-6408

Campaign Women's Conference (network of Democratic women campaign workers), c/o Women's Voices, 1112-16th Street, N.W., Suite 750, Washington D.C. 20036; telephone (202) 822-8060

CAWP News and Notes, Center for the American Woman and Politics, Eagleton Institute of Politics, Rutgers University, New Brunswick, NJ 08901; telephone (908) 828-2210

Common Cause, 2030 M Street, N.W., Washington, D.C. 20036; telephone (202) 833-1200

Federal Communications Commission, Broadcast Bureau, 1919 M Street, N.W., Washington, D. C. 20554; telephone (202) 632-7586

Federal Elections Commission, 1325 K Street, N.W., Washington, D.C. 20463; telephone (800) 424-9530

Fund Raising Institute, 12300 Twinbrook Parkway, Suite 450, Rockville, MD 20852; telephone (800) 877-TAFT

Fund Raising School, Indiana University Center on Philanthropy, 550 West North Street, Suite 301, Indianapolis, IN 46202; telephone (317) 274-7063

League of Women Voters of the United States, 1730 M Street N.W., Washington, D.C. 20036; telephone (202) 429-1965

NARAL, National Abortion Rights Action League, 1101 14th Street, N.W., 5th Floor, Washington, D.C. 20005; telephone (202) 371-0779

National Black Women's Political Leadership Caucus, 3005 Bladensburg Road, N.E., Suite 217, Washington, D.C. 20018; telephone (202) 529-2806

National Women's Mailing List, P.O. Box 68, Jenner, CA 95450; telephone (707) 632-5763

COMPUTER SOFTWARE

Questionnaire Programming Language (QPL), software program which allows individuals to conduct interviews or surveys by phone by providing the caller with appropriate questions to ask and allowing instantaneous entry of responses. Complete set (software, manuals, and a demonstration disk) for $150 (order # PB90-501545, Version 2.0); manuals alone for $23 (order # PB90-501552, Version 2.0); demonstration disk alone for $15 (order # PB89-131551). Sales Desk, NTIS, U.S. Dept. of Commerce, 5285 Port Royal Road, Springfield, VA 22161; phone (703) 487-4650.

PC File 5.0 (List price $149 but available through mail order houses for $99 or less); Database software suitable for campaign use, reviewed in *Campaigns & Elections* magazine, January 1988; Editor's Choice by June 1990 PC Magazine; Available at list price from ButtonWare, Box 96058, Bellevue, WA 98009; telephone 1-800/J-BUTTON.

File-Maker II (List price $225 but available through mail order houses for less) database software for MacIntosh computers.

D-BASE IV (List price $795 but available through mail order houses for $499 or less), well-known database software.

Other database programs available off the shelf or by mail, see current issues of any computer magazine.

MS Word, Word Perfect, MacWrite, PC-Write, Word Star, Volkswriter, etc., various list prices, all well-known word-processing programs widely available.

Also see current editions of *Campaigns & Elections* magazine and *Campaign* magazine for advertisements for campaign software and current editions of various computer magazines for other database and word processing software.

WOMEN'S PACs (POLITICAL ACTION COMMITTEES)

For a list of Women's PACS, write:

CAWP News and Notes, Center for the American Woman and Politics, Eagleton Institute of Politics, Rutgers University, New Brunswick, NJ 08901; telephone (908) 828-2210

EMILY's List (Supports pro-choice Democratic women candidates for congressional and gubernatorial office); 1112 16th Street, N.W., Suite 750, Washington, D.C. 20036; telephone (202) 887-1957

NOW Equality PAC (National Organization for Women, non-partisan, supports progressive women candidates for federal, state, and local office), 1000 16th Street, N.W., Suite 700, Washington, D.C. 20036; telephone (202) 331-0066

NWPC PAC (National Women's Political Caucus, bipartisan, supports progressive women candidates for federal, state, and local office); 1275 K Street, N.W., Suite 750, Washington, D.C. 20005; telephone (202) 898-1100

Women's Campaign Fund (Bipartisan, supports progressive women candidates for federal, state, and local office); 1601 Connecticut Avenue N.W., Suite 800, Washington, D.C. 20009; telephone (202) 234-3700

NATIONAL CHOICE PACs

NARAL PAC (Bipartisan, supports pro-choice male and female candidates and pro-choice ballot measures); 1101 14th St. N.W., Washington, D.C. 20005; telephone (202) 408-4600

PRO-CHOICE AMERICA (Supports pro-choice male and female Republican candidates), P.O. Box 18866, Washington, D.C. 20036-8866

REPUBLICANS FOR CHOICE (Supports pro-choice Republican male and female candidates); 1315 Duke Street, Suite 201, Alexandria, VA 22314; telephone (703) 836-8907

VOTERS FOR CHOICE/FRIENDS OF FAMILY PLANNING (Bipartisan, supports pro-choice male and female candidates, mostly for congressional and legislative races); 2000 P Street N.W., Suite 515, Washington, D.C. 20036; telephone (202) 822-6640

INDEX

More Tips for Getting Elected and Getting Things Done RIGHT!

101 Campaign Tips for Women Candidates and Their Staffs by Jewel Lansing

Need more help getting elected? This is THE book! "101 Tips" offers hard-nosed practical advice you'll need to run an effective campaign—you and your staff will find this an invaluable resource.

$9.95   Order #886

Want to Solve Problems?
Easy • Fast • Effective

You can with "The Solution Strategy" by Phil McWilliams! You will be shown step-by-step how to solve any problem. This book is being used by smart leaders everywhere! Let it work for you!

$9.95   #875

❖ ❖ ❖ ❖ ❖ ❖ ❖ ❖ ❖ ❖ ❖ ❖ ❖

Give Speeches and Presentations Like A Pro!

The *Presentation Handbook* by John Carrington-Musci is the most dynamic book available to teach you how you can give effective presentations.

Be A Top Performer!

$14.95   #872

❖ ❖ ❖ ❖ ❖ ❖ ❖ ❖ ❖ ❖ ❖ ❖ ❖

"Campaigning For Office: A Woman Runs" by Jewel Lansing

Insightful information for anyone running for office or anyone wanting to learn what it's like from the inside of a campaign.

$9.95   #887

❖ ❖ ❖ ❖ ❖ ❖ ❖ ❖ ❖ ❖ ❖ ❖ ❖

Want to be a Super Leader???

Will Clark's "The Leadership Handbook" gives you 101 effective ways you can shine as a leader. Learn how to lead, what gets results, what to avoid, how to motivate an individual or an entire organization. **A Real Powerhouse of IDEAS!**

$14.95   #814